WINTER

in the

WILDERNESS

WINTER

in the

WILDERNESS

A FIELD GUIDE TO

Primitive Survival Skills

DAVE HALL *with* JON ULRICH

Comstock Publishing Associates

A DIVISION OF

CORNELL UNIVERSITY PRESS

ITHACA AND LONDON

Illustrations by Dave Hall.

First published 2015 by Cornell University Press
First printing, Cornell Paperbacks, 2015

Printed in the United States of America

Design by Scott Levine

Library of Congress Cataloging-in-Publication Data

Hall, Dave, 1968– author, illustrator.
  Winter in the wilderness : a field guide to primitive survival skills / Dave Hall with Jon Ulrich.
    pages cm
    Includes bibliographical references and index.
    ISBN 978-0-8014-7995-3 (pbk. : alk. paper)
    1. Wilderness survival—Handbooks, manuals, etc. 2. Snow camping—Handbooks, manuals, etc. I. Ulrich, Jon, 1976– author. II. Title.
    GV200.5.H35 2015
    613.6'9—dc23
                            2015010559

Cornell University Press strives to use environmentally responsible suppliers and materials to the fullest extent possible in the publishing of its books. Such materials include vegetable-based, low-VOC inks and acid-free papers that are recycled, totally chlorine-free, or partly composed of nonwood fibers. For further information, visit our website at www.cornellpress.cornell.edu.

Paperback printing   10 9 8 7 6 5 4 3 2 1

To Lily

I am honored to have been
a part of your journey

I went to the woods because I wished to live deliberately,

to front only the essential facts of life,

and see if I could not learn what it had to teach,

and not, when I came to die, discover that I had not lived.

Henry David Thoreau, *Walden*

Contents

Acknowledgments

A book is never the work of one or two people. We thank the following individuals for their tireless support of, and dedication to, this project.

I would like to start by thanking all the youth and families with whom I have worked over these many years. I especially want to acknowledge the amazing participants who were there from the beginning and were part of so many winter adventures: Lily, Estelle, Emily, Megan, Connor, Zach (the Mule), Brian, Adam, Sam, Savanah, and Greg. I also thank Linda Schoffel for being an awesome supervisor. Thanks to all the Primitive Pursuits staff members with whom I have worked over the years, especially Tim Drake, Jed Jordan, Beth Bannister, Heidi Bardy, and Dave Muska. You guys are the best.

Thank you to my friends, Jeff and Sue, for all your assistance during countless winter overnights. A special thanks to Kevin Clarke and David Werier for their guidance with this project. To my dear friend Tom Liebler, who saved my ass so many years ago—thanks, Bait. Thank you to everyone at Cornell University Press—especially Kitty, Peter, Karen, Jamie, and Emily.

To my sister and parents: You have always encouraged me in all my endeavors. Thank you so much for all that you have done.

To my loving, wonderful, and supportive family: Thank you, Jacob and Aron, for all your help over the years building and experimenting with snow shelters. Thank you so much to my beautiful wife, Sharon, who always lets me get away on my crazy adventures. I love you all so much.

Last but not least, I thank Jon for being the best guy in the world to work with. This book wouldn't have happened without you.

Dave Hall

▼▼▼

I thank Kitty (for all the late-night e-mails), Peter, Karen, Jamie, and all the wonderful people at Cornell University Press. I also thank my loving family—Laura, Graham, and Elliott—for the accommodations they made over the years this book was written. To my parents, thank you for cheering us on every step of the way. Last, I thank Dave for the opportunity to contribute to such a pioneering work.

Jon Ulrich

WINTER

in the

WILDERNESS

Introduction

It was a cold still afternoon with a hard steely sky
overhead. . . . The country lay bare and entirely leafless around
him, and he thought that he had never seen so far and so
intimately into the insides of things as on that winter day when
Nature was deep in her annual slumber . . . He liked the country un-
decorated, hard, and stripped of its finery.

Kenneth Grahame, *The Wind in the Willows*

It's fifteen degrees outside, there's over two feet of snow on the ground, and I'm laughing. I've pulled an amateur move and have begun to sweat inside my snow shelter. I know better. I've entered my snow trench headfirst, and in an effort to turn around so I can close my door, I've overheated. I could have exited my shelter and come in feetfirst, but in an act of stubbornness I've defied rational thought. Staying as dry as possible in a winter survival situation is one of the cardinal rules.

I'm leading a winter overnight into the wilds of central New York with a group of high school students. Our goal is for each person to solo in his or her own shelter without the aid of a sleeping bag or blanket. I'm joined by my coworker Tom Archibald (a rookie in matters of winter survival) and my good friend Suzanne Johnson. Sue has been to many of Tom Brown Jr.'s Tracker School classes, including a winter survival intensive. Both Tom and Sue use sleeping bags. The rest of us go without.

The students I've invited on this challenge are prepared. They've been practicing survival skills for years and have become well versed and comfortable in wilderness settings. Some have even become instructors for Primitive Pursuits, an outdoor education program I founded in 1999 in the town of Dryden.

I emerge the next morning unscathed. For one thing, I'm wearing a sensible combination of wool and synthetics, allowing me to stay warm despite the moisture. Second, I exited my shelter and was able to regulate air flow through my layers and dry out before settling down. Later in the evening, when I found myself unable to sleep, I joined several students around the fire.

Still, my situation is a telling reminder of how quickly fortune can turn on even the most seasoned outdoorsman. One misstep could mean the difference between life and death.

Why Winter Survival?

My immersion in winter survival began more than twenty years ago as a natural extension of my interest in primitive skills. As an instructor, I knew I could not ignore this topic if I wanted to build confidence while exploring the outdoors. Because the driving force behind primitive survival is that all of our needs can be met through a deep and meaningful relationship with the earth, it was necessary that I learn to meet these needs without the aid of gear or technology.

The purpose of this book is to go beyond the fundamentals of winter survival and introduce readers to this relationship. In this way, the idea of spending a night outdoors during the cold season can be met not with fear but with excitement and anticipation. Through a detailed explanation of what the body requires, you will learn to flourish under such conditions.

Shelter, of course, is a primary concern, and here readers will develop an understanding of what shelters are best suited for their particular situation. This book will also examine the "native" or ancestral approach to meeting one's needs. This approach to wilderness survival strives to reconnect us with skills that are independent of modern gadgetry. Such relationships run deep and are a rewarding way to interact with our world.

To quote Samuel Thayer, "The dominant conception of Western environmentalism is one of detached appreciation. We need a new paradigm—one of attachment and participation."[1]

Reclaiming "Nativeness"

Imagine a bushman tracking in the savanna, eating plants that he has long known and sleeping in a thatched hut. Without the benefit of technology, the fundamentals of creating warmth, fashioning shelter, obtaining safe drinking water, and finding food are acquired through practices that have been mastered and knowledge that has been attained over time.

This process, which I refer to as reclaiming one's "nativeness," is for most of us a forgotten birthright. This becomes not survival as most people think of it (surmounting the odds under do-or-die circumstances) but a way of living and relating to the earth that is peaceful and harmonious. With that said, I advise you to ease yourself into this process, particularly when it comes to the winter months. Always keep safety in the forefront of your mind. Although I'm a proponent of learning ancestral skills, I also acknowledge the value of modern survival techniques. Learning is a process. I encourage my students to focus on core fundamentals before moving on to more advanced skills.

Learning winter survival has not only enhanced my affinity with nature but has illustrated that we can all learn to assimilate these skills into our lives. Anyone, even the most seasoned outdoorsman, can become stranded in a vehicle or disoriented while hunting. Mother Nature is unforgiving; she is an indifferent force. Learning how to respect her power, maximize your efficiency, and avoid critical mistakes can make all the difference. So it is for two reasons that I write this book: to enrich and empower those who spend time in the outdoors and to help save lives.

In my own work teaching primitive skills, I often ask new students what they would need to ensure their survival for a night, a few days, or even a month. It should come as no surprise that, in a society where food is so abundant, the majority of students consider the acquisition of sustenance a top priority. In truth, the average person can go for weeks without food, putting this need at the bottom of our list in the initial stages of any crisis.

One thing that provides comfort within the context of a winter survival situation, or any survival situation, is the idea that if you honor and understand your priorities, your chances of persevering increase. The warmer months allow for greater flexibility in terms of how you spend your time, and although your body's needs are the same, the implications of not meeting these needs during the winter can have devastating consequences.

The Modern Paradox: Survival versus Camping

There is a great movement in America today whereby thousands of people are taking deliberate steps to reclaim ancestral skills. Our forebears relied on these skills to meet their most basic and fundamental needs. Many enjoy camping in a primitive style, meaning that they practice and apply this knowledge to realistic situations for which they are well suited.

Although primitive living is different from camping, there is often a melding of both disciplines. I have found that I do this myself—I may bring along food so I can focus my efforts on shelter construction or bring a sleeping pad so I can invest more time in trapping. My friend and colleague Tim Drake has said that the best time to practice survival skills is before you need them. In doing so, you will be prepared for any emerging crises.

People often venture into the wilderness with the aid of modern gear. I take a cautious approach to the topic of modern gear—it enables us to travel to interesting, out-of-the-way places, but it can also provide us with a false sense of security. There are few of us in the Western world who have grown up living within nature's daily rhythms. We no longer make our homes in shelters of bark and sod. We no longer forage for wild edibles. And we no longer have a respect and understanding for the powers of nature.

Although we have distanced ourselves from nature and consider it outside the sphere of modern existence, we are drawn to adventure, to hunt and travel in wild spaces. And herein lies the paradox: our ancestral drive is in no way tempered by an innate knowledge of primitive skills. Without establishing an intimate relationship with the earth, one can easily get into trouble. Gear can fail. Natural resources pass by unnoticed. Useful skills are underutilized. And tragedy often ensues.

Global Climate Change

According to the Intergovernmental Panel on Climate Change (IPCC), "Warming of the climate system is unequivocal."[2] But that doesn't necessarily mean less snow. Scientists have deduced that human activity has influenced shifts in global climate patterns, and as a consequence we are now seeing more extreme weather events in the form of hurricanes, flooding, drought, and—you guessed it—winter storms.[3]

The consumption of fossil fuels combined with deforestation has led to an increase in the release of carbon dioxide into the atmosphere.[4] In fact, the amount of carbon dioxide in our atmosphere has reached unprecedented levels—more than four hundred parts per million. This is the highest levels have been in more than 2.5 million years.[5]

What does this mean for the winter survivalist? In addition to unpredictable weather patterns, warming trends may make hypothermia all the more likely—cold rain and slushy conditions are far more detrimental to a hiker's well-being than powdery snow.

Still, colder temperatures are not a thing of the past. In January of 2014 winter storm Hercules dropped more than a foot of snow in parts of the Northeast, with temperatures falling below zero.[6] That same month winter storm Leon crippled parts of the Deep South, as Louisiana and South Carolina declared states of emergency. Ice and snow brought traffic to a standstill, causing closures along Interstate 65 in Alabama.[7]

▼▼▼

How to Use this Book

I recommend reading this book in its entirety to fully grasp the concepts presented. At the end of each chapter, I have included exercises that are designed to encourage hands-on experience. It is imperative that all these skills first be mastered in a controlled setting. Indeed, it would be tragic to meet your demise in a winter survival situation having only digested the contents of this book. Think of it as the difference between reading about playing the piano and actually placing your hands on the instrument.

Gradually introducing the skills presented in this book while on a "modern" winter outing can be a fun way to develop your confidence. One example of this would be to set up a tent for peace of mind but to build one of the many snow shelters depicted in these pages. Another way to ease into this process would be to master the use of a friction fire device with the intention of procuring flame but to bring along matches for added security.

I also encourage practicing "backyard" survival. This means treating your backyard, state park, or nearest wild space as the real deal, retreating to the comfort of your home or vehicle only if necessary. I have made numerous snow shelters in my backyard and have hosted many survival outings on my property. For beginners, close proximity to a warm, indoor space can provide a much-needed boost to morale.

Finding a group of like-minded people who share your enthusiasm is another way to become proficient in these skills. I'm fortunate in that I have a community of friends who adore going out into the woods with limited gear. Having others to learn from and bounce ideas off of is an invaluable resource.

Consider this book a wilderness companion—it should accompany you on outings and be regarded as a trusted friend. It is now my intention to share with you what I've learned over my almost quarter-century in the field.

Welcome to a new way of enjoying winter.

Chapter 1

Priorities

> An extended stay in the wilderness inevitably directs one's attention outward as much as inward, and it is impossible to live off the land without developing both a subtle understanding of, and a strong emotional bond with, the land and all it holds.

Jon Krakauer, *Into the Wild*

When I was in college, I went whitewater kayaking in Letchworth State Park in western New York State with my good friend, Tom Liebler. I was a novice, having navigated local creeks and rivers only during the summer. This particular trip took place on a beautiful fall day, and we were excited about the journey ahead. I was dressed for the occasion, outfitted in jeans, a sweater, and my finest dock shoes.

Before launching, a woman with a paddling group reprimanded me for my lack of attire. "You have no business being out there," she said with an air of contempt. Tom and I dismissed her comments with a shrug and headed off down the Genesee River.

The gorge was captivating. Splashes of color peppered the landscape as sunlight illuminated the mountains of shale towering before us. Without warning, the waters narrowed and we paddled through a series of standing waves. In an instant I was drenched. I began to shiver as Tom and I pulled off onto a shaded sandbar. In the throes of panic, my body became rigid and my brain went numb.

Tom, who was protected by a waterproof top, soon realized I was hypothermic. Although I had dry clothes, energy-rich food, and matches in my backpack, I didn't have the presence of mind to act. Fortunately, Tom did. He removed my clothing, provided me with sustenance, and nursed me back to a state of consciousness. Had I been alone, I could have easily wandered off in a daze and found myself on the precipice of death.

In retrospect, taking the necessary precautions was all that was needed to ensure my safety. Careful planning and proper execution would have all but guaranteed my survival.

Avoiding Panic

It's been said that the most important survival tool is the mind. The ability to maintain your composure in the face of adversity will do more for you than even the most sought-after gear. The best way to avoid panic is to understand your priorities, stay focused, and act in accordance with the situation. Panic erodes once survival skills have been mastered. This confidence comes not from reading or observation, but from what I refer to as "dirt time," or genuine hands-on experience. By practicing these skills in a controlled setting (meaning you have a secondary plan if necessary), you will gradually add more and more options to your repertoire.

For many of my beginning students a backpack full of gear is mandatory, but as time passes and their proficiency increases I often let them decide what they're going to bring into the woods. In many cases, this becomes nothing more than the clothing on their backs.

Asking "What If?" Questions

It seems like yesterday that my journey into winter survival began. I, along with my friend and colleague Tim Drake, wondered if we could safely lead a group of middle school–aged youth into the wilds of central New York. (We had of course developed a backup plan—if necessary we would retreat to the comfort of my heated workshop, which was only ten minutes away.) This became the first of dozens of winter survival experiences, some of which are detailed in these pages.

Much like Tom Brown, Jr., I always encourage my students to ask "what if?" questions with regard to survival.[1] These fundamental questions are important regardless of the situation and include: "What if I need to get out of the wind?" "What if I can't find water?" "What if there isn't anything to eat?" When people ask these questions, it demonstrates that they are considering the bigger picture and actively seeking to fill in any gaps in their skill set.

The most important of these questions during a winter survival situation is "What, if anything, can I do to stay warm?"

Hypothermia and Frostbite

In January of 2013 an Illinois man, David Decareaux, and his two sons, Dominic and Grant, set out for a hike in Missouri's Ozark Mountains. Although the temperature at the outset was in the fifties, rain quickly moved into the area, and temperatures plunged into the twenties. Their bodies, outfitted in light gear, were found on a bluff the next day, dead from exposure to freezing temperatures.[2]

In most instances, those who perish in wilderness situations do so not from starvation or dehydration but from hypothermia. This is true no matter what the season—exposure claims more lives than any other factor. According to the Mayo Clinic, constant shivering is a key sign of hypothermia. Other symptoms of moderate to severe hypothermia include

- Lack of coordination
- Slurred speech
- Stumbling
- Confusion
- Poor decision making
- Drowsiness
- Apathy

- Progressive loss of consciousness
- Weak pulse
- Slow, shallow breathing[3]

Because the average person can survive three to four weeks without it, finding food isn't something you need to spend a lot of time on in the initial hours of a survival situation. On the other hand, people have been known to succumb to the elements in as little as a few hours under exposure to harsh conditions. It is therefore crucial that you understand your priorities to make the most efficient use of your time. In certain situations there is no margin for error.

Let's begin by assessing your core temperature. For most, this is approximately 98.6 degrees Fahrenheit. If you are poorly insulated or otherwise lacking protection from the elements, this core temperature may begin to drop. We have all experienced the first stages of hypothermia in the form of shivering. In an effort to warm itself, the body vibrates. The resulting friction creates heat. This shivering is your body's way of communicating danger, a warning you must heed before the more advanced stages of hypothermia take hold.

Do not mistake hypothermia for frostbite. You do so at your own peril. Frostbite is injury to the body's tissues as the result of exposure to extreme cold. Although painful, it is not as devastating as hypothermia. You can help avoid frostbite by covering exposed parts of the body such as the nose, fingers, and toes, as these extremities are often the first to be claimed by low temperatures.

At the first signs of hypothermia, you must take action. Your situation and the resources at your disposal will best determine your course of action. The important thing is to act quickly. A few points to remember:

- Get out of wet clothes and into dry clothes.
- Escape from the wind.
- Remain active (be careful with this—without adequate caloric intake, you will deplete valuable energy).
- Get into the sun.

- Move up off the valley floor where cold air accumulates, and avoid direct contact with rocks or snow (if you need to sit down, use a barrier such as brush or other insulation).
- Build a fire and fashion shelter.
- Consume energy-rich foods (such as nuts) and warm liquids.

Variables that might induce or exacerbate hypothermia include

- Inadequate, damp, or wet attire
- Cold temperatures
- Malnourishment
- Wind
- Contact with cold surfaces

Clothing is your first (and in some cases your only) defense against the elements. Simply put, it is your primary shelter. It is for this reason that you must carefully consider your choice of attire.

Clothing and Attire

In the winter of 2010 Tim and I guided a group of twenty-one students from the State University of New York's College of Environmental Science and Forestry through an overnight in Morgan Hill State Forest in Truxton, New York. We trusted that college-age students would understand the importance of our gear list, but we were mistaken. Half of the group had donned woolens, synthetic layers, fleece, and appropriate footwear. The other half, however, were outfitted in nothing but jeans, noninsulated hiking boots, and cotton. We spoke to the group about our concerns and goals for the excursion. Fortunately our camp was a ten-minute walk from the parking area, and we knew that students could be escorted to an idling van if necessary.

At camp, my colleague and I built several miniature snow shelters, discussing the benefits and drawbacks of each. Students were encouraged to break into groups and build whichever shelter they preferred. All went well for the first few hours. When Tim and I were not working on our own shelter, we helped others and offered advice. Around midday it began to snow, then sleet, and then rain.

We'd started a fire earlier in the day using a pump drill. Everyone was drawn to the comfort and heat it provided, as rain soaked us from the shoulders down. I unpacked my "heat sheet," which offered protection from the elements and worked well as a fire reflector. When we kept this emergency blanket over our heads, our situation improved. I even had to shed layers to keep from sweating.

For those who didn't have the benefit of a reflector sheet, the fire was enough to keep them warm. After the better part of an hour, the rain let up and we started the long process of drying out. Those who were dressed in cotton quickly changed into dry attire. It was so cold that a pair of wet jeans that were left unattended were found frozen stiff the next morning. The fire made our survival possible.

Tim and I stayed by the fire the entire night. Our original plan was to sleep in a snow tepee without sleeping bags or blankets, which we had done many times before. Even though we had built a wonderful shelter with a superb bed, the most comfortable place was next to the fire.

Of the twenty-one students, thirteen used their shelters for the night. This particular storm was responsible for the closing of many roads in the area. Conditions made travel treacherous, and downed trees caused local power outages.

Your choice of clothing will determine whether you start a survival situation at an advantage or disadvantage. Potentially life-threatening circumstances may not be life-threatening at all if you have proper attire. Avoid cotton at all costs. In Primitive Pursuits, we refer to this as "death cloth." Cotton absorbs water and, when wet, will quickly cause your body to cool. Synthetic and woolen layers are a much better alternative and will keep you warm even if you become damp.

You will also want to avoid sweating. Instead of one or two heavy layers, it's best to have several layers of lighter material that can be added or removed as needed to maintain a comfortable temperature. Once or twice

I've neglected to remove layers only to begin sweating. When I cooled off, I ended up with ice between my layers of clothing. Remain vigilant and stay as dry as possible.

Synthetics are wonderful in that they are soft, warm, and lightweight. Nylon outerwear sheds snow and makes an excellent windbreaker. Synthetics, however, are not as durable as wool, and if you spend time around a fire you will inevitably end up with small holes from sparks. If I know I'm going to be around fire, I wear outside layers of wool. This natural fiber is indispensable.

When it comes to gloves and mittens, invest in material that's strong. I've owned many expensive pairs of synthetic gloves and mittens made by brand-name companies. These products always end up ripped and torn. Meant primarily for skiing and mountaineering, they often fail within one day of branch collecting. I therefore recommend a layered approach to keep your hands warm. I use an insulated leather glove inside an insulated leather mitten. This leather mitten should be waxed and waterproofed, and can be found at most farm and garden stores. A layered approach enables you to remove the mittens when you need more dexterity or to avoid sweating.

▲▲▲▲

13

I use a natural beeswax product to waterproof my mittens. One problem with leather is that if it gets wet, it can take a while to dry. If my gloves are damp, I prefer to wear them when I'm using a fire to dry them. This prevents the gloves from getting too hot, which may cause them to shrink, crack, or harden. (Wearing your gloves, as opposed to leaving them by the fire, alerts you to when they are becoming too hot.) Synthetic overmittens can be added as well. These should have a durable palm and be long enough to cover a good portion of your arm. I use overmittens whenever I'm working with snow.

Although much of your clothing can be purchased at thrift stores, I don't recommend this for boots. I've been wearing the same pair of La-Crosse footwear for over twenty years. These are specifically designed for use in cold temperatures. Winter boots need to have removable liners. These liners can even be worn inside sleeping bags and dried by the fire if necessary. Insulated rubber bottoms with leather triple-stitched uppers are ideal. Go with a tried-and-true brand name boot that is rated to handle the extreme temperatures you're likely to encounter. Nothing's worse than cold feet.

I also use gaiters. A gaiter is a sleeve of synthetic material that covers the lower part of your leg to just above your ankle going over your boots. Gaiters keep snow from collecting under your pant legs and, most important, keep it from entering the tops of your boots.

Hats are also essential, as heat is lost disproportionately through the head. Scarves or neck warmers should be added to your arsenal of clothing not only to insulate but to protect against frostbite. Headwear can be layered just like any other area of the body. I've had as many as three layers on my head, including a good synthetic hat, a balaclava, and a hood.

Down is another insulator that's lightweight and easily transported. I love my down sweater and jacket. There's nothing like the warmth down provides, but it can be rendered useless if it becomes wet. Ensure that these outer garments are sized to fit comfortably over your other layers.

Waterproof yet breathable materials are available in both top and bottom layers. As with any outer layer, make sure these are sized generously.

The art of learning primitive survival skills is in and of itself a "layered" practice. Indigenous peoples of the North Country used skins and furs to maintain warmth. Although this book will not address this topic, the committed survivalist may wish to embark on a study of hide tanning. For those of you not inclined to take this leap, store-bought articles can be bolstered with the addition of vegetation.

Many native cultures used materials such as dried grasses and sedges inside footwear and clothing to add insulation. For those who are inadequately dressed, this can be an effective technique. Simply stuff dry, insulated material into your pants and shirt (with your cuffs tied off). Even headwear can be insulated by adding grasses. My friends Tim, Jed, and Suzanne did this on a memorable outing in the Pepperbox Wilderness Area of Adirondack Park, New York. With stuffed outfits and a leaf crib (see chapter 3), they were able to maintain significant warmth during a multiple-night outing.

Worst-Case Scenarios and the Importance of Fire

The ability to employ fire as part of your survival strategy is vital. As a precaution, I always carry at least two modern means of procuring fire (a handheld lighter and a sparking tool) when venturing into the backcountry. Beyond providing warmth, fire can be used to cook, boil water, and signal. Fire is the one skill that must be mastered if you hope to surmount the most hostile conditions.

In a winter survival situation, fire is your second priority. (Proper attire, of course, takes precedence above all else.) Although water is essential, you will need fire to heat cold water or to melt snow and ice. Not only will cold water rob your body of precious calories, but it may contain harmful parasites and bacteria or even induce hypothermia. A fire with a reflector will save you when nothing else—even shelter—can. I cannot overemphasize the importance of fire. Although your course of action will be dictated by the weather and resources at your disposal, fire often means the difference between life and death.

▲▲▲▲

15

Our ancestors had a foundational sense of the weather and would hole up around the fire when things became harsh. In modern society we've become less in tune with the pulse of nature, foolishly venturing out on foot into oncoming storms. Although snow is formidable, melting snow and rain are even more detrimental to your well-being. Such conditions can quickly lead to wet clothing, hypothermia, or death. Effective shelters are difficult to create during these times. Mastery of fire is therefore necessary to assure survival. I'm a strong proponent of primitive methods, but modern fire-making devices also have their place.

I have long considered worst-case scenarios. When it comes to winter survival, this doesn't mean snow or even subzero temperatures. On the contrary, ample snow means shelter and cold temperatures mean low humidity. The most dangerous wintertime situations involve temperatures that hover around the freezing mark and include slush or rain.

▼▼▼

Shelter

Shelter, which will enable you to maintain warmth over an extended period of time, is your third priority. Believe it or not, snow may hold the key to saving your life in a winter survival situation. When used effectively, a variety of snow shelters can be created that will keep you warm and protected from wind and precipitation. I have found that snow shelters are superior to tents during winter outings. A basic understanding of how to work with snow is crucial in learning how to create the proper shelter.

Water

After your core temperature is stabilized, the body requires an ample supply of warm, drinkable water. To function at an optimal level, it is recommended that you consume a minimum of four quarts of water a day. One piece of advice I offer my students is to monitor the color of your urine. If you void your bladder and your urine is a dark yellow color, you're dehydrated. If, however, your urine is clear, you can rest assured that you are adequately hydrated.

Sustenance

Our ancestors of the North Country made sure they had enough food to safeguard against the winter season. This was a thoughtful and intentioned process. To assure their survival, they stowed their annual harvests.

Procuring adequate sustenance during the winter can indeed be a difficult task. Whereas in the summer there are a great variety of edibles, this simply isn't the case during other times of the year. Any and all calories obtained through hunting, trapping, and foraging will be welcome to the winter survivalist. Not only will this stem weight loss, but under ideal circumstances you may even maintain your weight. Because meat is a calorie-dense food, you must become an expert trapper—I have yet to meet anyone (myself included) who is skilled enough to secure two to three thousand calories a day within the context of a winter survival situation.

Helpful Crafts and Skills

The accumulated knowledge of our ancestral past is boundless. In my work, I have focused on learning skills that help me meet my immediate needs in the most expeditious way possible. In chapter 6 I will delve into those crafts and skills that are most applicable to winter survival situations.

Navigation and Orienteering

Learning to navigate effectively is another important skill that anyone venturing into the backcountry should come to know intimately. Although it's important to know how to use modern navigational tools such as maps, compasses, and global positioning system (GPS) units, it's equally important to understand the art of aidless navigation. Such techniques will prevent you from getting lost in the first place and help you make intelligent choices should the need to walk out of a survival situation arise.

An understanding of what it takes to keep your body fit is essential to wilderness survival, and knowing your priorities will help determine the most important course of action, thereby eliminating the loss of precious time and energy. The chapters in this book are prioritized according to needs specific to the winter season, and it is for this reason that fire appears first.

Chapter 2

Fire

The red glow moved from the sparks themselves into the bark, moved
and grew and became worms, glowing red worms that crawled up
the bark hairs and caught other threads of bark and grew until there
was a pocket of red as big as a quarter, a glowing red coal of heat.

Gary Paulsen, *Hatchet*

During one particularly memorable group outing, I set the goal
for each of my participants to make his or her own shelter. We had excellent snow for this event and constructed a series of quinzees (snow shelters)
in a semicircle, completing the other half of the circle with a bench that
doubled as a reflector wall.

I challenged one of my more adroit participants, to whom this book
is dedicated, to hold off on building her shelter until four that afternoon.
Not one to remain idle, she and another female participant fashioned a
two-person cord drill from hemlock branches found near our camp. Using
a shoelace for cordage, they soon produced a coal. The resulting fire was
an absolute godsend, as it provided warmth for periods of the night when
we were unable to sleep.

The body's ability to maintain heat is crucial to survival. Under certain
conditions, hypothermia can paralyze the survivalist in a matter of minutes. Fortunately, there are many things you can do to prevent your body
from losing heat. Environmental conditions and available resources will

always determine the best course of action. Above all else, one must proceed with haste.

Because of situations involving moisture, crafting a rudimentary shelter such as a snow cave might exacerbate your situation. The ability to create and manipulate fire to serve your needs is therefore of paramount importance. In this chapter you will learn to

- Start and maintain a one-match fire
- Maintain and set up a smart fire with a reflector wall
- Fashion cordage (rope)
- Employ primitive fire-starting methods
- Use fire as a tool (creating bowls and heating rocks)
- Carry fire

Fire adopts a magical quality when created via primitive means. When a spindle rotates back and forth against a board to create an ember, its beauty almost defies description. Seeing a glowing ember placed inside a tinder bundle and coaxed into flame is a transformative experience. Fire does many things:

- Provides warmth and enables you to work with your bare hands
- Heats and purifies water
- Dries clothing
- Cooks food
- Creates vital crafts and tools
- Heats rocks
- Wards off insects
- Provides companionship

▼▼▼

Location

In Jack London's seminal short story "To Build a Fire," an unnamed protagonist trudges across the frozen Yukon wilderness in search of refuge. Panic-stricken after falling through the ice and sinking in water halfway to his knees, he attempts to produce a flame. In his urgency to find warmth, the man builds his fire beneath a spruce tree. As he is about the remove his moccasins, disaster strikes—snow from the overhanging boughs, which had been disturbed by his presence, falls toward the earth, suffocating his fire.

Before we embark on a discussion of how to make fire, it is imperative that you understand the importance of location. Always choose a safe, sensible place—one that is well drained, in close proximity to fuel, and free from wind. Be sure to stay clear of trees to avoid damage to root systems (this will also diminish the risk of underground fires). Keep in mind, too, that your flame could ignite low-hanging branches. Any branches laden with snow might also drip or collapse onto your fire.

Do your best to scrape away any snow cover and get as close to the ground as possible. Failure to do so will result in a pooling of snowmelt around your fire, which could easily neutralize your efforts. As an added precaution, build your fire on a layer of bark or branches to keep it off the ground during its initial stages of growth.

In windy conditions, look for places that offer some form of protection. This might mean moving to the lee of a hill or mountain, finding solace behind a natural feature such as a root ball, or building a lean-to to serve as a wind break. Without some sort of break or reflector, your fuel will burn quickly and much of the heat your produce will be misspent.

Assuming the ground isn't frozen, remove the organic duff layer from your site and ring your fire with dirt or nonsedimentary rocks. Remember to fully extinguish your fire before moving on to another location, covering it with soil and camouflaging your site. Unless you are in a true survival situation, leave not a trace of your activity. (Evidence of your whereabouts, of course, will aid search and rescue efforts.)

Modern Methods

In terms of modern fire making, there are many devices available. Some of these are suspect, and some I wouldn't be caught dead without. Whatever you choose, be sure you become proficient with it under the most unfavorable conditions. I like handheld lighters (which those of us in Primitive Pursuits refer to as the "thumb drill") and have a penchant for magnesium sticks with built-in strikers. Using a knife, scrape off a pile of shavings from your magnesium stick. Then make sparks using the built-in sparking rod. If all goes well, your magnesium will soon ignite. The best way to capitalize on this flame is to have punky wood, birch bark, or small twigs available. Once lit, your birch bark or twigs can be placed under fine twigs or a lean-to structure.

Another option is a sparking tool. This unit is lightweight and can be affixed to your keychain. The metal scraper, which is attached by a piece of cordage, throws off a hot spark when scraped along the sparking rod. This will ignite dry leaves, birch bark, and punk with ease.

On sunny days you can even use a magnifying glass to encourage punky wood to smolder. The trick is to hold the magnifier so that it's square to the sun in an effort to create the smallest, roundest point of light possible.

Starting a Fire

When you are practicing with matches, I'd recommend learning to make fire under the most adverse conditions imaginable. If it's raining, get out there! If the forest is covered in ice and the wind is blowing, get out there! Fire is hardest to produce when you need it most.

If you've practiced this all-important skill, you'll be well versed and in a much better position to succeed when the need arises. With primitive methods, however, I would suggest experimenting under more ideal circumstances. First, I'll examine three tried-and-true methods for producing flame with a match or lighter when conditions are moist.

Carving

Inside every dead branch is dry wood. All wet bark and outer wood can be stripped with a knife, and the remaining dry wood can be carved into thin, long strips. The key to getting a fire going with twigs or wood carved into splinters is to think small. Most inexperienced fire makers begin with wood that is much too large. It is best to have different stages of kindling available before lighting your twigs to avoid losing any flame you produce.

Splinter Sticks

Remarkably, even in a downpour dry splinters can be obtained from various species of trees and bushes. Experiment by breaking dead branches to determine which ones splinter (as opposed to which break clean) when you bend them. These inner splinters can be gathered in mass quantities. This is an essential skill to master, particularly in cold but rainy conditions. I have even used green splinters to successfully ignite fires.

23

Tinder Bundles

Tinder bundles comprise materials culled from the wild that enable you to induce flame from a coal. Materials suitable for making tinder bundles include buffed grasses, the downy material from seed and flower heads, and the inner bark from trees and plants.

This material should be dry and fibrous. Regardless of what material you ultimately choose, be sure to buff and twist it to the point that it becomes soft and fine. Although I prefer tinder bundles derived from the inner bark of cedar trees, there are a number of materials, such as dried goldenrod leaves, that are well suited for this purpose. (It is important to note, however, that cattail down must be mixed with other tinder materials to ignite.)

When gathering tinder, create a robin's-nest-shaped bundle and then gently place your ember inside. Using your bundle to envelop the coal, exhale into the center of your nest. If your bundle is tightly compressed, it might suffocate your coal. Conversely, if your bundle is too loose, any heat that's created may not have the opportunity to proliferate. This process is one that can be mastered only through practice.

In damp or moist conditions, locating tinder may prove difficult. Here are a few suggestions that will help ensure your success:

- When you identify quality tinder, place it in an inside pocket to help shield it from the elements. Keeping a healthy supply of tinder on your person is a good habit to develop.
- Using a coal extender in companion with your tinder bundle is another way to increase the likelihood of success. When added in small quantities to tinder, materials such as punky wood, certain polypore fungi, and chaga maximize the chances that your bundle will ignite once you place a coal inside. (Polypores are also known as "bracket fungi" and are typically found on dead or decaying trees.)

When the heat from your coal comes into contact with a coal extender, this material will begin to glow red and your ember will grow in intensity. With a focused stream of air, tinder bundles—with an added boost from coal-extending materials—are often quite successful.

The Lean-to Fire

Adopt the mind-set that you need to be able to produce a fire with one match. A simple way to organize your fire is to construct a lean-to. To create the lean-to, lay tinder such as hemlock twigs or dried garlic mustard against a small log. (This material should be fine and wispy—about the diameter of a toothpick.) This simple method keeps your fuel off the ground and enables oxygen to feed the flame. It is also quite stable. To light the lean-to, simply place your flame underneath or place a flaming tinder bundle into the hollow. As your fire grows, you must be prepared to add additional fuel. Planning ahead by collecting various stages of kindling

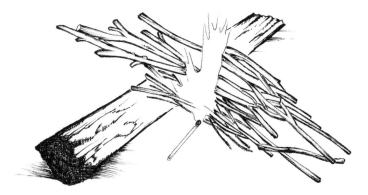

The lean-to structure enables oxygen to feed your flame.

and other fuel will prove indispensable. Start with more twigs, gradually crossing them over your fire and adding larger and larger twigs and
branches. Again, remember to think small.

It's important to understand why the lean-to is so effective. Because
of its design, air can easily pass beneath your structure. When you light
your lean-to, do so from beneath so that the flame travels up toward your
fuel. When I use a "fire burrito" in companion with the lean-to, I place the
almost-lit burrito next to a small log, lay fine, flammable materials across
the top, and encourage it with a steady stream of air.

As this material starts to burn, it's important to engage with your fire.
This is a critical point in the life of your flame. Your fire can easily go out
if you don't add proper fuel. Begin by adding small twigs, moving next
to pencil-width fuel, and gradually increasing size as your fire grows in
intensity.

Once your lean-to fire is ablaze, you've bought yourself added security.
It will be up to you to maintain and use your fire judiciously. In a true
survival situation, a large fire may be what keeps you warm throughout
the night. The ends of large-diameter logs can be placed on your fire in a
spoke or star pattern. As this large-scale fuel burns, the ends can be pushed

toward the center to ensure a steady supply of fuel.

Keep your fire-making materials in a dry place such as an inside jacket pocket. It is also advisable to have a healthy supply of these materials in your shelter should you need them.

Be sure to keep your fire organized and be deliberate about placement. Above all, fire needs three things to proliferate: a heat source, fuel, and oxygen. If any of these is absent, your fire will not burn efficiently. Novices often make the mistake of building a fire that's flat, meaning all their fuel ends up on the ground with little to no space in between. In such instances, oxygen will have a difficult time reaching your fuel, and the fire will suffer as a result. Keep your wood "fluffy"—you don't want your fuel to be too far apart or too close together. Once a bed of coals is established, larger pieces of wood (even logs) can be added. When practicing, be conservative. Hone your skills, but save the larger fires for when you need them most.

Punky Wood and the Fire Burrito

This is my preferred method of fire making in inclement weather. It can be used with modern techniques as well as more primitive methods. The fire burrito requires three things to ignite: punky wood, bark, and twigs or splinter sticks. Punky wood can be extracted from rotting trees (deadwood). At some point between the time when a tree dies and the time it decomposes it may reach a state of ideal punkiness. Look for trees that have been ravaged by woodpeckers—a good indication that punky wood may be present.

This wood is light, easily crumbled between the fingers, and often a bit spongy. In the Northeast, I most often look to beech, maple, and birch trees. Even in rainy or icy conditions, dry, punky wood can be found beneath a damp or wet exterior. This is a highly combustible material. What I like to do is crumble the punk onto a slab of bark, insert a small smoldering piece of punk, and add more chunks of punk. I then cover this with a handful of twigs and put a bark lid on top.

If performed correctly, more often than not this setup will turn into flame with no further action on your behalf. (In fact, I've had fire burritos that were difficult to extinguish!) To expedite the process and ensure that your ember punk grows, simply blow through one end of the burrito. The bark roof helps create a hot microenvironment and protects against precipitation. Practice this method until it is mastered. You'll be amazed at how quickly your ember ignites.

Preserving Fire

Even if you've created a shelter that doesn't require the use of a fire to maintain warmth, you will still want to preserve embers with which to work. The following methods will aid you in keeping your fire ablaze.

Ash and Soil

One way to extend the life of your fire is to cover your smoldering wood in a layer of ash or dry soil. As with all survival skills, this should be practiced to the point that you can guarantee you will have red-hot embers to unearth the next morning. A few inches of ash or soil is all that's required to preserve your coals overnight.

On many occasions, after spending a night inside a snow cave, I have emerged in the morning to find smoldering logs that were easily coaxed into flame. Still, it is best to leave nothing to chance when trying to preserve this valuable resource.

The "Upside-Down" Fire

Another way to quell the burning process is to build what is known as an "upside-down" fire. This method, which originated in Europe, has been around for centuries. First, build a log-cabin-style structure. I build my upside-down fires with wood that is approximately two feet in length and two inches in diameter. Although the dimensions of the finished product should resemble a two-foot cube, there's room for experimentation. (Because wood

27

The upside-down fire is lit from above.

in the wilderness is never perfectly sized, I tend to place my thicker pieces on the bottom and progressively build up with smaller pieces.)

Unlike most fires, the upside-down fire is lit from the top. Build a small tepee on top of your structure with solid kindling. As the fire burns, it will slowly drop coals onto the wood below. This is a wonderful technique to master, as it helps you learn to control the rate at which your fire burns. If you are using a fire and lean-to for warmth, this method may diminish the need for you to get up as often during the night.

Spiral Punk

Punky wood can also be used to light your lean-to in a controlled fashion. Sticks of punk are laid in a spiral pattern so that they overlap one another (envision a circular row of toppled dominoes). The outermost end of punk is then lit. The smoldering slowly travels around the circle, each piece igniting the next. In the center of your arrangement will be a burrito/lean-to hybrid that has been built up with an ample supply of fuel. If all goes well, you'll have fire waiting for you when you wake up the next day.

Cordage

One thing you can't be without in a survival situation is cordage (rope). This is a critical component of the bow drill and two-person cord drill. When time is of the essence, shoestrings are the most readily available (and often overlooked) type of cordage. (Be sure to test your shoelace's fortitude before using it on a drill—you don't want to be without fire *and* snug footwear!) And although a snow-covered landscape makes the process of unearthing suitable materials formidable, nature offers a multitude of options. It should be noted that cordage can also be made from materials not resilient enough for use with friction sets.

Spruce Roots

Spruce roots can be found near the earth's surface. Begin by scratching for these with a sharpened stick under the base of the tree. Pull these roots to the surface, exercising the utmost care to avoid breaks. Spruce roots work best when split and with the outer bark (or skin) removed. Splitting takes practice. Begin the split with a knife or sharp rock and pull the two halves apart. If one side becomes thinner, pull slightly downward on this half, and it should head back toward an even thickness. Spruce roots work best with the two-person cord drill and should be bent with the fingers or worked over a smooth branch before use to ensure pliability. These are used by simply wrapping your spindle so the rounded, outer portion of the root is exposed. *In trials, this material withstood a fifty-pound test.*

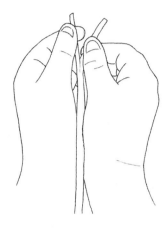

**Harvesting spruce roots is
an effective means of
acquiring cordage.**

Hickory Branch Bark

Hickory branch bark is best harvested from the small limbs and branches
of the hickory tree and should be between one and two inches in diameter.
Using a soft, rounded rock, tap the limb against a flat surface to loosen
the bark, exercising care to avoid damage. Then use a knife or sharp rock
to split the bark at the base. Gently peel back the bark the length of the
branch. *In trials, this material withstood a one hundred-pound test.*

Dogbane

Dogbane, if found without rot (black or darkened areas), makes excep-
tionally strong cordage. This member of the milkweed family can be plentiful in winter, as it has a tendency to proliferate in fields and meadows.
To harvest the outer skin, break the shafts in half lengthwise by applying
pressure with your hands against a flat surface. The woody interior will
in turn break into segments, which can be removed as the skin is peeled
away. *In trials, this material withstood a fifty-pound test.*

▼▼▼

Making Cordage

Now that you have your materials, you'll need to fashion them into something useful. One method I employ is known as the "reverse-wrap." This takes patience to learn, but much like knitting or crocheting becomes second nature with practice. Certain materials work best if moistened, affording them greater flexibility.

First, pinch the material into a tight loop between the thumb and index finger of your left hand, making sure one end is slightly longer than the other. (This will enable you to weave in splices with greater ease if necessary.) Pinch the top portion of the remaining material between the thumb and index finger of your right hand (holding it only an inch or so from your left hand) and turn it away from your body. Using the middle finger of your right hand, grasp the lower portion of the material and twist both strands toward you. What had been the lower strand will now be at

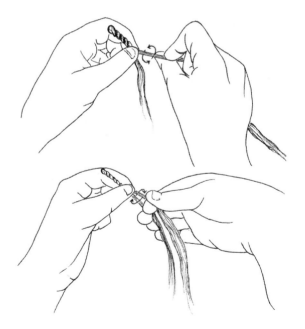

With practice, the reverse-wrap will become second nature.

the top. Repeat these steps until you have produced a cord. Keeping the twist tight, slowly inch your hands down the length of the cord. When you are first learning the reverse-wrap, it is beneficial to practice with different colors of jute twine, tied together at one end, to better visualize the process.

Primitive Fire Making

Although I cannot overemphasize the importance of carrying several modern fire-starting devices with you when venturing into the wilderness (e.g., matches, lighters, magnesium sticks), circumstances may not afford you such luxuries. Learning to make fire the ancestral way is powerful and can foster a strong sense of confidence. Fortunately there are dozens of ancestral methods for making fire, and learning these techniques will deepen your appreciation for nature. In this section I will discuss those fire-making methods that I have found most reliable during the winter months.

Here we'll examine three methods used to make fire by primitive means—the bow drill, the two-person cord drill, and the hand drill. All three utilize a spindle and notched baseboard (also known as a fireboard) to produce a coal. A dark dust will accumulate in the notch of your baseboard as the spindle rotates and downward pressure is applied. The resulting ember can be coaxed into a flame using a tinder bundle or coal extender such as punky wood.

Before you attempt to fashion a coal, I'd advise putting a wood shaving or a dry leaf underneath your notch as a catch. Once an ember is produced, there's no need to rush. If your notch is filled with dust and smoking on its own, it will become more solid if you give it a few moments to rest. I prefer to give my baseboard a firm tap before I move it out of the way. This tap will release the ember from the board so that it stays on your catch. Now that your coal is separate from the board, it can be transferred to a tinder bundle or placed on punky wood.

Certain woods produce the best results. Although I would recommend using cedar for the spindle and baseboard (cedar is difficult to master and therefore encourages proper form), the following woods are suitable for use with the bow drill and two-person cord drill: cottonwood, willow, aspen, alder, birch, beech, sassafras, sycamore, tamarack, and juniper. You would do well to avoid hardwoods such as maple, as well as conifers including pine, spruce, and firs. Pine pitch, however, makes a wonderful lubricant for your handhold.

For the hand drill I favor sumac, willow, cottonwood, cedar, poplar, or box elder for the baseboard. The drill itself should be lightweight and slender. For this I prefer yucca, mullein, burdock, fleabane, aster, ragweed, goldenrod, horseweed, or evening primrose.

A fresh kit with all its component parts has neither a socket in the handhold nor a notched socket in the baseboard. When first building your kits, you will need to "burn in," meaning create these sockets. With the bow drill and two-person cord drill, begin with a spindle that has pointed tips (this will resemble a short dowel—about eight to twelve inches in length and three-fourths inch thick—that is tapered at both ends). Bore a small depression into the center of your handhold and baseboard with a knife or sharp rock. Ideally the socket on your baseboard will be about a half-inch from the edge; you can then add a triangular-shaped notch, which should be an angle of about forty-five degrees.

Once the socket in your handhold is burned in to your satisfaction, it will need lubrication (pine pitch, evergreen needles, and nuts work well, as do oils from the skin and hair). Without lubrication, your handhold will continue to burn. Be mindful of which end of the spindle meets your handhold, as this will need to be lubricated. Remember to protect your kit from wet and snowy conditions. Keep it covered when traveling, and work on a slab of bark if necessary.

Now we'll look at the differences between these three methods.

The Bow Drill

The bow drill comprises four main components: the bow, handhold, spindle, and baseboard. One of the more challenging aspects of the bow drill is fashioning the bow's cord. This cord, if not man-made, can be difficult

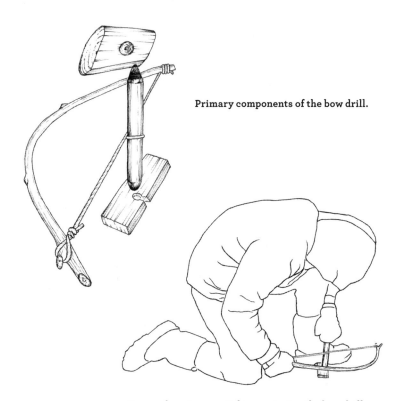

Primary components of the bow drill.

Proper form is essential to mastering the bow drill.

to produce in a winter situation. With proper form, this technique is relatively simple to master. First, wrap the cord around the spindle. Place your left foot on the baseboard so that your instep is about an inch from your notch, and kneel on your right knee. Carefully place the spindle between the handhold (which will be in your left hand) and the baseboard. Apply downward pressure to the handhold, bracing your arm against the outside of your left leg. Quickly draw the bow back and forth the length of the string with your right hand, being sure to keep the bow level. Dust will collect and the notch will begin to smoke. If all goes well, the dust will begin to smolder, indicating that you have produced a coal. If you are left-handed, simply reverse this process.

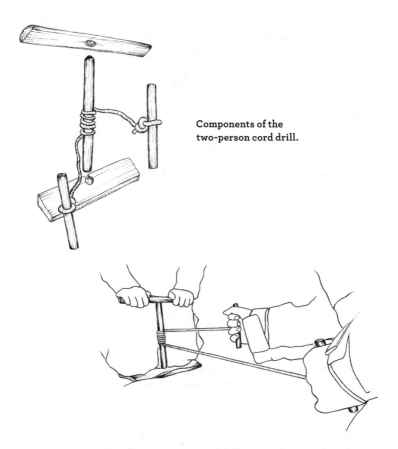

Components of the
two-person cord drill.

For the two-person cord drill, one person steadies
the spindle while the other drives the cord.

The Two-Person Cord Drill

The two-person cord drill is similar to the bow drill except that it takes—
surprise—two people. The first person kneels on the baseboard, steadies
the spindle, and adds downward pressure while holding an elongated
handhold. The second person is the engine. A sturdy cord (ideally three
feet in length) is wrapped around the spindle approximately six times.
The ends of the cord are held in each hand and pulled back and forth.

The second person must use long pulls and take care not to tangle the cord. Make sure that you don't allow the cord to go slack. (To avoid tangling, keep your right hand high and left hand low, or vice versa.) Once the drill is running smoothly, a coal will appear in the notched baseboard.

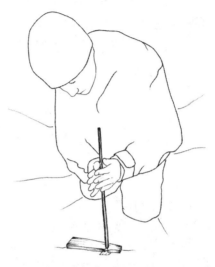

Once the technique is mastered, the hand drill will usually produce a coal in fewer than five passes.

The Hand Drill

The hand drill is the easiest of the three methods to understand but the most difficult to execute. It can be painful on the hands in cold weather. This elegant device requires only two components—a drill and a baseboard. The drill comprises a tall, thin, dead plant such as horseweed or goldenrod. Smooth down your drill with a knife or rock to make the drilling process easier on your hands. I like a drill that is somewhere between fourteen and twenty-four inches in length. This drill should be thick enough so that your palms don't rub together during the spinning process, and the board should be as thick as the diameter of your drill.

When you are learning this method, it's important to stop practicing before blisters develop. If you feel spots starting to form, it's best to stop for a day or two and let your hands recover. For this method, your hands should start at the top of the drill. Imagine that you're pushing in on the spindle. This will prevent your hands from traveling down the shaft too quickly. Rub your hands back and forth. Although some prefer to use the whole hand, I'm more comfortable using my palms. As you drill, apply downward pressure. Your hands will move down and end near the baseboard. Quickly move your hands back to the top of the spindle, exercising care to keep your drill in contact with the board. I typically produce a coal with the hand drill in three to five passes. With practice, you will learn to love the hand drill.

Fire as Tool

Historically, the uses for fire have gone well beyond heating and cooking. In terms of winter survival, one of the most important uses for fire is in the purification of water. In the absence of a metal container, fire can even be used to create coal-burned wood bowls as vessels to boil water. A coal-burned vessel is simply a log or hunk of wood that has been burned to create a catch. This process is simple, but as with all primitive skills it requires practice.

If a saw and ax are available, a log that is free of knots and checks can be split in half, and coals can be placed on the flat surface. The trick with this method is to avoid allowing your coals to flame up. Coals are easy to control, while in comparison flames will lick over the edge of your container and burn the side of your catch. Once you're satisfied with the depth and size of your bowl, you can scrape the charred interior clean with a rounded rock or stick. (For more about coal-burned bowls, see chapter 6.)

Water can be heated or boiled in your coal-burned bowl with hot rocks. Look for nonglassy, nonsedimentary rocks. Granite is ideal, as sedimentary and glassy rocks may explode. If you're unsure if the rocks you've selected are safe, place them in your fire and create a distance of at least fifty feet between yourself and the flame. Once the fire has started to abate, the rocks should be safe to handle. If your rocks are hot enough (often they will be glowing red), it will take only a few egg-sized pieces to boil a liter of water. Stews and teas can be made using this method.

Heated rocks can also be tucked into clothing and brush beds and used as hand warmers. Exercise caution to ensure you don't burn yourself or light your shelter on fire. (For more about this, see chapter 3.)

Carrying Fire

The time may come when moving from your current location is necessary. The ability to bring fire with you on your journey is indispensable. Fortunately, this skill is easily acquired once you've become familiar with punky wood. Long sticks of punk can be carried with you while you travel (I often travel with two as a precaution). This stick will eventually burn down. Before it gets too small, light another stick and continue on your way. Burning can be slowed by wrapping your punk in bark. (This helps control the amount of oxygen it receives.) Be careful not to drop any embers while you walk if you're doing this in nonsnowy conditions.

Chaga

Chaga, or *Inonotus obliquus*, is a fungus, irregular in shape and with the appearance of charred wood, that grows primarily on birch trees and is also known as "clinker polypore."[1] I have used it in several ways. First and foremost it is a coal extender, meaning that after I have produced a coal with a friction kit I can take the resulting ember and place it on a piece of chaga, being sure to keep the ember in contact with the interior orange-colored flesh. The dried chaga will quickly absorb heat from the coal and begin to smolder. This can then be added to a tinder bundle and enticed into a flame.

Second, chaga can be used to carry fire, although I prefer to use punky wood because it's more plentiful. Chaga can have various densities, even within a single piece. This is important to note because it's possible that a dense piece of chaga may not take a coal easily, and larger pieces may be soft and spongy in the center. This soft and spongy material is especially useful when making fire with a traditional flint and steel kit or a modern sparking kit. Most chaga will take a spark, but the spongy interior is especially potent.

One novel use of chaga is as a baseboard in your friction kit. Drilling directly onto this material can produce a coal—that is, the chaga itself will begin to smolder (no notch is required). I have done this with all three of the aforementioned friction fire methods, although it does take a bit more elbow grease to get your chaga to ignite than to produce a coal with a notched baseboard.

Exercises

1. Practice making fire with two man-made mechanisms (e.g., magnesium sticks, matches, lighters) in all kinds of weather—especially wet, cold, or snowy conditions. Your objective should ultimately be to gather materials and light a fire in fewer than five minutes.

2. Fashion all three primitive fire-making devices described above. Become accomplished in each of these methods, eventually taking them into natural areas and attempting to create fire. As an added challenge, fashion cordage from natural materials and use this with the bow drill and two-person cord drill.

3. Learn to properly identify punky wood. Gather this, along with other coal-extending materials, and make fire using the burrito method. In addition, experiment with carrying fire for extended periods using punky wood, tinder fungus (chaga), or other materials that smolder (e.g., shelf fungus). Practice wrapping your materials in bark to slow the burning process.

Chapter 3

Shelter

I had made my hemlock bed right in the stream valley where
the wind drained down from the cold mountaintop. . . . I was right
on the main highway of the cold winds as they tore down upon the
valley below. I didn't have enough hemlock boughs under me, and
before I had my head down, my stomach was cold and damp.

Jean Craighead George, *My Side of the Mountain*

In February of 2012, Saratoga Springs attorney Steve Mastaitis
became separated from his hiking party after summiting Mount Marcy
in the High Peaks of the Adirondacks. After veering from the trail, he
continued down the mountain until he found himself near a steep ledge.
"It was treacherous," he later recalled. "I was afraid to take another step."

Although he succeeded in reaching emergency personnel on his cell
phone, Mastaitis soon realized that he would have to spend the night on
the mountain. All efforts to light a fire proved fruitless. Shelter was his
only hope for survival.

In an act of resourcefulness, Mastaitis hand-dug a snow cave, punch-
ing through the ice with his fist. "I didn't stop moving," he said. "I didn't
want to fall asleep."

Mastaitis emerged from his shelter at sunrise. At around 8:30 a.m. he
heard voices in the distance. Forest Rangers had located his position. Although hypothermic and frostbitten, he was alive.[1]

Water in the form of snow crystals can be manipulated and sculpted for
use in a variety of shelters that not only are easy to build but create space

superior to the finest winter tent. A well-constructed snow shelter represents security, refuge, and contentment. I have wonderful memories of the dozens of nights spent sleeping in snow shelters, having sooloed, slept out with my children and friends, and accompanied myriad youth from the Primitive Pursuits program.

A well-built snow shelter will

- ▲ Insulate. A snow shelter can have inside temperatures well above freezing—even when outside temperatures are below zero.
- ▲ Protect you from wind. Convection, conduction, and radiation are the primary means through which the body loses heat. Because the inside of a properly built snow shelter is still, there is little heat lost as a result of these factors. High winds can otherwise make for a cold night.
- ▲ Create quiet space. The inside of a snow shelter is incredibly serene, allowing for quality sleep.

I have spent wonderful, calm nights inside snow shelters while storms raged outside. I once sooloed inside a large, structured snow shelter. With straw as my bedding and a wool blanket, I enjoyed an excellent night's sleep. In the morning, I worked inside my shelter without the aid of gloves. When I was ready to leave, I was surprised to learn that the doorway had drifted in, making it necessary to dig out. The winds outside were fierce. I jogged home through temperatures that, with the wind chill, were well below zero. The blowing snow caused near whiteout conditions. Without my shelter, it would have been a difficult night indeed.

Types of Snow

Before embarking on a discussion of shelters, let's examine the one common building material: snow.

Snow comes in many disparate forms. It has been said that the Saami people of northern Europe have almost two hundred words for snow in its various states.[2] In the Western world, we tend to use adjectives when we talk about snow, characterizing it in terms such as powdery, sugary, wet, slushy, compacted, old, or crusty.

Powdery snow is dry and fluffy. To the casual observer, it may seem like a poor material with which to build a shelter. But for the winter camper and survivalist, powder snow changes into something solid that can be dug into when it has been moved either by wind or people and left to sit for an hour or two.

As winds drift snow across an open field, it will collect at slopes and natural barriers in the landscape. Drifted snow can be a great place to build a snow trench. Areas where drifted snow ages and becomes compacted are also great places to carve out snow pits and caves. Aged drifts, as well as windblown snow that has aged (think arctic conditions), present wonderful opportunities to quarry blocks for igloos and block shelters. When powdery snow is unaffected by wind, it can be made useful once it is moved and shoveled into piles.

▲▲▲▲

43

The longer a drift or pile is allowed to sit, the more suitable it will be for quarrying or excavating. Bottom layers of snow, by virtue of the pressure exerted on them from above by upper layers, are compressed into more manageable material. In arctic regions, snow from both upper and lower layers may be of use because of the absence of variations in temperature, which enable the snow to rest for greater periods of time.

Snow, of course, can come in other forms. Wet snow, the stuff that makes great snowballs, occurs when temperatures are at or above thirty-two degrees Fahrenheit (or when temperatures are just below freezing but snow is exposed to direct sunlight). Large, snowman-sized snowballs can be rolled with wet snow and used to create shelters.

"Sugar," or corn snow, is more like icy pellets. This material, which is less cooperative than powder, can still be moved, tamped down, and left to sit. Any blocks that are quarried from sugar snow piles can be brittle and are best suited for a structured snow shelter, in which a brush-covered frame holds the insulating layer of snow, creating a hollow core.

Tools of the Trade

When it comes to improvised tools, the survivalist needs to identify anything he can that will move snow. This may mean something as simple as collecting snow with your feet. This method is a bit tiresome, but it works. Jackets can be used to carry snow (a tarp is even better). Your jacket should be cold and made of nylon so the snow doesn't melt or cling. You can kick or place the snow on the jacket and then move it to your shelter pile. Anything that can aid in digging and piling snow can be useful. Other examples include canoe paddles, cooking pans, and hubcaps.

As for natural options, one can turn to bark slabs and sticks. There are students in the Primitive Pursuits program whom I have challenged to construct snow caves using only sticks and a mitted hand. Sticks are a wonderful tool for quarrying blocks out of drifts. Through experimentation, you may even discover your own tools.

Commonalities of Shelter Design

All basic survival shelters have several things in common despite their contrasting designs:

- Walls that are at least one foot thick
- A brush bed and, if time and resources allow, an insulated bed
- A closed doorway
- A useful interior
- An air hole or vent

Walls

One-foot-thick walls are the standard minimum thickness to maximize snow's insulating properties. For some shelters, such as quinzees and igloos, snow is the only building material used. These do not rely on internal beams or branches for roofing or structural integrity.

The Brush Bed

The brush bed is a necessity for a survival snow shelter. In its most rudimentary form, this is a pile of brush to keep the survivalist off the ground. Without a brush bed, the body will lose heat. As time and resources allow, building an insulated bed is the best option. This is a bed that goes beyond raising you off of the floor—it insulates and contains body heat much like a bed at home.

When snow caves are used for camping, be sure to use a quality sleeping pad designed for extreme conditions. Foam or self-inflating pads may be used, but many low-quality foam pads will crack and break in subzero temperatures.

Inside a snow cave, you may use a pile of brush to lie or sit on. In certain situations, time is of the essence if wind or whiteout conditions are closing in. Avoiding direct contact with the snow may be enough. In such cases, sit on a pack or pile up evergreen boughs as a place to sit. I have experimented with minimalist shelters to prove to myself that with a simple structure and a raised bed of piled sticks and brush, you can make it through the night without a blanket, sleeping bag, or additional natural insulation. Admittedly this will provide for a restless night, as I have always been too cold to sleep comfortably. To warm up, I exercised as best I could, doing stomach crunches while flexing my arms, legs, fingers, and toes.

Spending a night alone in the confines of a small cave made of snow can seem like an eternity. There is great comfort, however, in knowing that with minimal shelter, a quick bed, a door, and a vent, one can get through the night without incident. With even more time, the survivalist can find warmth and comfort by creating a proper bed of insulating materials, with further insulation being added as a makeshift blanket.

▲▲▲▲

45

▼▼▼

The Doorway

Over the years I've experimented with many door designs. Instructors with the Primitive Pursuits program have used giant snowballs and brush and once even rigged large chunks of snow to collapse and cover the entryway after our group was inside. A closed entryway is a critical component of any snow shelter. It is only by way of a properly closed entryway that a shelter gains the ability to insulate, keep blowing snow out, and become a refuge. I prefer a double-wall system made from blocks of snow.

With this system, the walls that close off the door are built once you're inside the shelter, and the blocks needed for construction are stored near the entrance area along the inner walls. After building the first wall and beginning the second (about six inches from the first), fill in the spaces between with loose snow. Your block walls will be imperfect, but placing loose snow between the walls eliminates unwanted drafts.

The Interior

For all practical purposes, the interior of your shelter will be the product of immediate needs, available resources, and time. Once the survivalist has met his or her basic needs, amenities may be added (for more details, see "Luxuries and Long-Term Considerations"). With patience and hard work, any shelter can be made into a comfortable home. Here are some things to consider with regard to your shelter's interior:

- ▲ A rounded or smoothed interior (this isn't compatible with all shelter types). This helps direct any melting toward the ground.
- ▲ An elevated platform or sleeping area above the floor (cold air sinks and warm air rises).
- ▲ A bathroom. (This may sound odd, but it beats getting up, opening your door, and going outside during the night.)
- ▲ An insulated bed.
- ▲ A covered entryway. This will ensure that your doorway remains open in the event of high winds or additional accumulation.

Ventilation

Sometimes you want drafts, and if so, you will need a means to control them. A quick note on drafts: on rare occasions, it may be necessary to vent your shelter to cool its internal temperature and prevent excessive melting. With shelters such as quinzees that feature a domed interior, this is not as much of an issue. Flat-roof shelters such as the quinzee trench, however, are more prone to dripping. Purposeful venting helps guarantee that your air stays fresh and that your shelter doesn't become too warm. Flat-roof shelters are easy to build and are the best choice in certain situations, but they can have one major consequence: if temperatures inside your shelter are above the freezing mark, your roof may drip. Venting your shelter will help it stay near the freezing mark. Domed shelters, those that have curved or arched interiors, are better equipped to handle temperatures above freezing. Any moisture that occurs tends to run down the interior walls to the ground.

Ventilation is also important in addressing the risk of suffocation. I would encourage making a hole in your roof roughly two inches in diameter, as this ensures proper oxygen exchange with the outdoors. In fact, I often keep a stick or ski pole next to me in the event that snow (precipitation, drift, or melt) covers my hole. Because of the risk of asphyxiation, I also discourage bringing fire into your shelter. Torches, candles, lighters, and matches consume oxygen and could potentially set any bedding materials ablaze.

Basic Dimensions

Basic dimensions start with the minimum—as a general rule, small is beautiful, but your shelter must be large enough to accommodate your needs. The survivalist never wants to sit, lie, or lean directly in the snow. Ideally, shelters should be big enough to allow you to move without brushing into the walls.

▼▼▼

Location

I have built shelters in all kinds of locations—edges of wetlands, woodlands, and open meadows. Location is often attributed to resources. I will choose one spot over another if it is close to insulating grasses and beams. Snow depth is also an important consideration, as are direct sunlight, wind, and potential hazards (areas prone to rock slides, flooding, or avalanches). I often look to set up camps near natural springs.

In addition to the need to be in close proximity to resources, it is important to keep the "shelter-within-a-shelter" concept in mind. Even though a well-constructed snow shelter will protect you from the elements, remember that you will likely be spending a good deal of time outside your shelter. It is for this reason that you should choose a sheltered area in which to build, meaning a place that gets adequate sunlight but is free from wind. Avoid mountaintops and places where cold air settles (valleys and ravines).

To quote Tom Brown Jr., "A good shelter in a bad location is a bad shelter."[3] It is best to heed this advice.

Tenants

If you leave your shelter unattended for stretches at a time, you are likely to encounter an unwanted tenant. At best this is comical, but at worst you could be in for a dangerous surprise. Over the years I have had all manner of wildlife take up residence in my shelters, including mice, deer, opossums, rabbits, and foxes. The most astonishing visit, however, took place during the writing of this book.

One winter's day some friends and I backpacked into a local state forest to admire a lean-to that had been constructed by one of our adult apprenticeship groups. As we approached our destination, I noticed an odd set of tracks leading into (but not out of) the shelter. I tiptoed over to the mouth of the lean-to, reached with my camera into the entrance, and snapped a quick photograph. Before I could wager a guess as to what had moved in, a porcupine darted out of the shelter and across the snow.

Types of Shelters

Although I will describe each type of snow shelter with which I have extensive experience, like any outdoorsman I have personal preferences and will opt for certain shelters over others. After discussing shelter types, I'll suggest additional features. With added time and resources, your shelter can become far more inhabitable. It is important to note that many of the concepts introduced in this chapter can be combined, yielding a vast array of hybrid shelters.

The Quinzee

The quinzee is a classic North Country shelter. It is made with nothing but snow and has no wooden frame or brush to reinforce its structural integrity. For this structure, powdery snow is first heaped into a pile. With the passage of time, it becomes something solid from which a hollow core is then excavated. The first time I slept in a quinzee was at a campground in Algonquin Park, Ontario, Canada. Even though it was April, the conditions were still winter-like, and several of these shelters had been built and left for others to use. These particular shelters had gone through a freezing and thawing process and had become more like ice houses. Despite being domes of ice, they served me and my friends well.

The process of building a quinzee is simple. Powdery snow is shoveled into a large domed pile approximately six to ten feet in diameter and five to seven feet tall. Because quinzees have no internal skeletal structure, they are best for groups of no more than three people (although I heard of a quinzee that was built for a group of thirteen!). Once the pile is complete, let it sit for at least an hour. (In colder temperatures, tamp down your pile and let it sit for as long as possible.)

This is the perfect time to collect bedding as well as an armload or two of straight sticks. Pincushion the shoveled snow with these sticks, inserting them to a depth of about twelve inches. The pile will resemble a porcupine, and the straight sticks will guide you in the excavation process. Once a quinzee pile has settled, it needs to be hollowed out to create a shelter, and these sticks will determine a healthy and proper wall thickness. From the

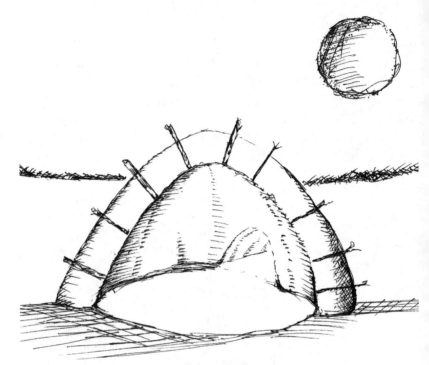

Cross-section of the quinzee.

inside, remove snow in any direction until you run into the end of one of these sticks. Once you hit the end of a stick, stop digging in that direction.

One of the drawbacks to the quinzee is the excavation process. Your pile needs to be hollowed, and this can be difficult. Snow, especially from the ceiling, will fall on you and potentially get you wet, cling to your clothes, and find its way down your neck. To minimize this problem, make the door wider than it needs to be. A larger door decreases the risk of getting cold or wet and helps expedite the excavation process. Once the inside is smooth and you've created a domed interior, this oversized doorway can be made smaller with blocks or a combination of sticks and blocks. This basic shelter can be embellished with a door or a bed (perhaps even a sleeping platform) to enhance your degree of comfort.

BENEFITS AND DRAWBACKS

Benefits
- ▲ Constructed entirely of snow. No auxiliary materials needed.
- ▲ The smooth-domed interior helps any snowmelt run down the walls.
- ▲ Great in areas with limited trees for resources.
- ▲ Low environmental impact.
- ▲ Can house up to three people, possibly more.

Drawbacks
- ▲ The builder can get cold or wet during the excavation process.
- ▲ Typically houses only three people comfortably.
- ▲ Usually sags within a few days.

A note about sagging: every quinzee I've built eventually sags and becomes uninhabitable within a period of three days. This may be attributed not to universal weather patterns but to climate variations in the Finger Lakes region of upstate New York. Consistent temperatures may therefore stabilize the quinzee. Allowing your pile to sit as long as possible before hollowing will promote your shelter's life. If you have the time and are not in immediate need of refuge, this will increase the snow's firmness. I have left quinzee piles for several days and found them almost impossible to penetrate. A cone shape, as opposed to a dome shape, may help avoid the sagging process.

The Snow Tepee

In wooded areas where dead trees and branches are available, the snow tepee is another attractive shelter option. This is my shelter of choice. The snow tepee is a quinzee with an internal frame that eliminates unsightly and inconvenient sagging. The frame is constructed using dead poles and branches and resembles a traditional Native American tepee. I prefer to use poles that are approximately one and a half to three inches

Dead beams comprise the snow tepee's internal frame.

in diameter, or wrist thickness. The finished interior will be a bit small-er than your standing wood frame, so be sure to keep this in mind. The peak, or point where the beams come together, is around seven to eight feet high. The top can be lashed together or, as is my preference, three poles with sturdy Ys can be locked together. Lean the remaining poles onto the frame to create your structure.

Once your frame is complete, fill the interior with snow until the beams are submerged to a depth of at least twelve inches. Be sure to cover the top of your tepee where all of the beams come together. As with the quinzee, let your pile sit and firm up for at least an hour while you collect bedding. With the snow tepee, there's no need to use straight sticks to determine wall thickness. Once you begin excavating the interior, you will start running into your beams. This is fine; these beams can show a bit. Think "cone" or "dome" while hollowing out your interior. Once it is smoothed and devoid of excess snow, your work on the main shelter is complete.

The snow tepee is an incredibly long-lasting and reliable shelter. The first shelter of this kind I built in my backyard. It lasted for weeks without sagging until it eventually melted during a late winter's thaw.

BENEFITS AND DRAWBACKS

Benefits
- ▲ The snow tepee is an exceptional choice when dead beams and branches are available.
- ▲ With both the quinzee and the snow tepee, the snow that is excavated from the interior can be piled along either side of the doorway to create a covered, trenched entryway.

Drawbacks
- ▲ As with the quinzee, one must be careful not to get wet during the excavation process.

▲▲▲▲
53

The Quinzee Trench

The quinzee trench is one of my favorite shelters. It's quick to build and is a model of efficiency and economy. An oval-shaped pile of snow is ideal. It doesn't need to be as high as that of a traditional quinzee, nor does it need to sit as long.

Collect beams, brush, and bark slabs while the pile rests for approximately forty-five minutes, and then shovel a trench through the middle of your pile. The snow you excavate should be kept nearby (this will become the roof) and should come out in large chunks or blocks. If it doesn't, this means the pile needs to sit for a longer period of time. Remove snow from your trench until you've created an elongated horseshoe-type shape that you can comfortably lie in. It should be a few feet longer than you are tall and wide enough that you have at least eight inches of space on either side. Using the beams you've collected and starting at the back end of the shelter, begin covering your roof. The beams should be long enough to rest solidly on the outside walls. Once you've worked a few feet, cover the beams with chunks of excavated snow. (Failing to cover the roof

The quinzee trench.

in segments will make it difficult to complete.)

Continue this process until you've covered the shelter from beginning to end. At this point, fill in any large gaps with small chunks of leftover snow. As a final step, throw a few inches of powdery snow over the top to ensure a well-covered roof that is at least twelve inches thick. Add a bed and create a door to complete your basic shelter. With extra effort you can make a pitched roof, whereby beams are shingled with bark or thatching. This will further prevent dripping.

BENEFITS AND DRAWBACKS

Benefits
- ▲ Efficiency of time and resources
- ▲ Can be built for two people
- ▲ Stability
- ▲ Easily modified for specific needs

Drawbacks
- ▲ A drippy ceiling is possible.

The downside of the quinzee trench is its flat roof. Any shelter that doesn't have a smooth, rounded interior can drip if temperatures rise above freezing. I have experienced significant dripping in the quinzee trench only once, when I spent a night outdoors with my oldest son. The temperature was five degrees outside, but our interior temperature was closer to forty. Our ceiling dripped mercilessly, and our sleeping bags became damp. I kicked open the door and pulled my son out of the shelter on the sled he was using as a bed. We finished the night in the open air. In retrospect, ventilating the shelter and allowing outside air to cool the interior would have alleviated any dripping.

The Snow Trench

When snow is deep enough or you find a suitable drift, you can easily craft a trench. This shelter is similar to the quinzee trench, the difference being that you identify a location where nature has created snow deep enough for you to dig a trench and thereby eliminate some shoveling.

BENEFITS AND DRAWBACKS

Same as the quinzee trench, but with the bonus of less shoveling.

Snow Caves and Pits

A quick shelter that may become necessary during a true survival situation is the snow pit. This is simply a small cave that has been excavated into a drift. The snow pit is a shelter that, with insulation to sit on and lean against, may be all you have time to build.

While you weather the night in your snow pit, you can let your imagination go and plan a larger, more comfortable shelter. This is the snow cave. With an arched roof and smooth interior, snow caves can be built to serve multiple inhabitants and include raised sleeping platforms and a covered entryway. Snow caves can be grand creations, as some drifts offer luxurious accommodations.

As with the quinzee, the builder has the potential to get wet and snowy during the excavation process. I recommend opening up your door wider than you'll need as you remove snow. This "working door" can be large enough to stand up in. Once your interior is sculpted to your satisfaction and all loose snow has been cleared, the entryway can be sealed using bricks of snow. Once this step is complete, you can cut a smaller, more reasonable-sized door through this wall.

Aged snow drifts offer excellent sheltering opportunities, but smaller and fresher drifts may present safety issues—while the bottom layers of a drift can be firm and dense, the upper portions may be loose. These layers do not facilitate the safe construction of snow caves and pits. Be aware of this as you're practicing. As you dig into drifts you will start to notice contrasting layers of impaction. Remain vigilant. Digging into weak snow can lead to cave-ins.

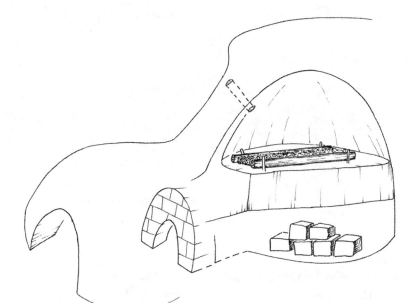

Snow caves can be built to serve multiple inhabitants.

In the Rocky Mountains of Colorado, the combination of high peaks and open country produces large drifts. In the Finger Lakes, three-quarters of our region is forested land. Drifts occur but not on the same scale. Learn to read your environment and practice snow pits and caves whenever possible. I've gathered most of my snow cave experience at the edge of a local football field, where an abrupt slope, open space, and regular winds have created drifts more than ten feet deep.

BENEFITS AND DRAWBACKS

Benefits
- ▲ Constructed entirely of snow.
- ▲ Domed interior prevents dripping.
- ▲ Lends itself to creativity and multiple rooms.

Drawbacks
- ▲ It is possible to get cold or wet during the excavation process.
- ▲ Potential issues with structural integrity, as upper portions of your drift may be prone to cave-ins.

The Structured Snow Shelter

The structured snow shelter is our program's default shelter when a large group needs to be under one roof for the night. Even though we've slept with as many as twenty-three people in one of these dwellings, it can be modified for smaller parties as well as the solo camper.

Craft a frame of sturdy beams to suit your group or individual needs. Little to no snow will get past your beams in the construction process, so you can get a good sense of your interior space while you're building. There is no standard frame design that is used for this shelter. For groups, we typically erect an elongated A-frame or a low-arched tepee-style frame. These types of frames can be sized as needed. For solo shelters, we've built debris-style frames (a small A-frame with one end of the ridge pole resting on the ground).

The structured snow shelter comprises a frame, lattice, and snow.

Once the frame is complete, collect a large amount of brush, grasses, weeds, and branches. This material will be used to create a latticework over your frame. With a structured snow shelter, the snow you put onto it stays out of the interior. It is the lattice that makes this possible.

If you're dealing with old or wet snow, covering your frame will be a cinch. Powdery snow, on the other hand, will sift through your lattice and end up in the interior of your shelter. To use powdery snow for the structured snow shelter, first move it into a large pile or a series of smaller piles. Once you have finished the frame, these piles will be solid enough to allow you to quarry blocks.

With proper bedding and a door these shelters are quite versatile. I've found that with a fresh snow covering, the structured snow shelter seems to gain strength as the added weight pushes down on the frame. These shelters will last until the next thaw.

BENEFITS AND DRAWBACKS

This brings us to the one problem with the structured snow shelter. Its interior, like that of the trench, is not a smooth, arched dome. The inner workings of your ceiling comprise beams, brush, and snow, and the snow layer is anything but smooth. If temperatures remain below freezing inside your shelter, this isn't a problem. When temperatures rise above freezing, however, the structured snow shelter may begin to drip as moisture travels down twigs and beams. Chunks of snow may even drop into the interior.

As with trench shelters, dripping can be managed in several ways. If outside temperatures are below freezing, ventilate. Another option is to use bark shingles or grass as thatching as a protective layer over your frame. Thatching, although helpful, can be a time-consuming process.

The Igloo

Many are familiar with the Eskimo igloo. A model of elegance and simplicity, it comprises nothing but blocks of aged snow. Because we don't have the same winters in the United States as are found in northern Canada, ideal conditions for quarrying igloo blocks, which come from windblown snow that has been allowed to age, are difficult to find.

On several occasions I have experimented with the igloo using wet snow packed into a recycling bin. I have also created ideal snow by leaving quinzee piles to sit for several days to quarry blocks. In a true survival situation when time is of the essence, the igloo is far from ideal.

The following diagrams illustrate a simple way of keeping your angles correct during igloo construction. This is one shelter where two or more people can be helpful. As the beveled blocks spiral upward and your structure becomes deeper, they can be supported from the inside until the final keystone block is cut and set into place. Loose snow is then tossed over the top of the igloo to fill in any spaces. To fashion a door, simply carve a rounded entrance into the side of your structure and use additional blocks to create a small, arched tunnel.

A tool that helps to make clean, flat edges is a necessity when it comes to igloo construction. I have used old carpentry saws as well as homemade wooden snow saws. Improvise and experiment.

BENEFITS AND DRAWBACKS

Benefits
- ▲ Constructed entirely of snow.
- ▲ Domed interior prevents dripping.

Drawbacks
- ▲ Construction is difficult to master.
- ▲ Proper snow conditions are virtually nonexistent in the continental United States (although suitable drifts may occur).

Snowball Shelters

One benefit of the snowball shelter is that it requires no tools. These are shelters that are constructed with damp snow, the same type used for making snowmen. I prefer a circular foundation, and I build up with more balls, slowly enclosing the roof. Because this can be tricky, I will sometimes use beams for stabilization to the point that I have a circular foundation that is several feet high. Visualize marking four points at the top of the foundation, and use beams to connect these dots. Now you have an internal framework that will support the snowballs as they are brought in to enclose the roof. After you've covered the first round of beams, repeat this process, eventually covering the shelter.

The snowball shelter has an irregular interior, meaning it isn't smooth and rounded and is prone to dripping if temperatures rise above the freezing mark. In an ideal situation, temperatures at night will fall below freezing, and a leaf crib can be integrated into your shelter plan.

▼▼▼

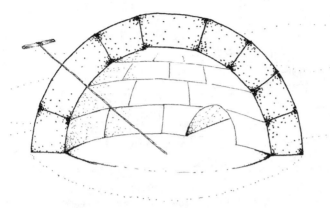

Cross-section of the igloo. A stake and cord can
help dictate proper angles during construction.

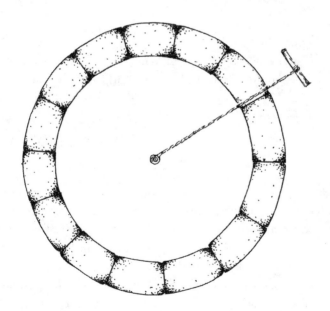

Igloo, bird's-eye view.

Snowball shelters are one option when working with damp snow.

BENEFITS AND DRAWBACKS

Benefits
- ▲ Efficient use of wet or moist snow.
- ▲ Interior can be smoothed to prevent dripping.

Drawbacks
- ▲ If temperatures stay above freezing, dripping is unavoidable.

Block Shelters

When snow conditions are inadequate or tools and experience don't lend themselves to igloo construction, block shelters can be a less elegant but effective alternative. I have built dozens of block shelters in and near my favorite drifts. Blocks of irregular size and shape can be quarried with a stick or mitted hand to create walls and an enclosed space. Although it is possible, getting the walls of a block shelter of this type to arch can be difficult. One way to expedite this process is to add beams.

Because of the jumbled nature of the block shelter, it will likely have gaps or holes. As a solution, stuff any large spaces with of chunks of snow. Before you consider your space finished, it's a good idea to cover your shelter with a layer of loose snow. This helps fill in small gaps and ensures that your walls are the proper thickness.

Beyond the challenge of closing in any gaps in your shelter's roof, block shelters have an irregular interior. This can become an issue if inside temperatures rise above thirty-two degrees.

BENEFITS AND DRAWBACKS

Benefits
- ▲ Constructed entirely of snow.
- ▲ Domed interior prevents dripping.

Drawbacks
- ▲ Ceiling prone to dripping.
- ▲ Closing the roof can be a challenge.

▲▲▲▲
63

Once completed, block shelters should be covered with a loose layer of snow to eliminate gaps.

The A-Frame Trench

This is a shelter that can be built into drifts with quarried blocks of snow. Learning to properly cut the blocks may take some practice. A partner can be of great value in helping set your blocks in place.

In order for this shelter to be successful, both the blocks and the trench itself must be cut from a solid drift of snow. Look for older, weathered drifts where you can quarry dense blocks. Unlike the snow trench, which uses beams to support snow on a flat roof, the A-frame trench uses only snow. The snow you choose must therefore have adequate structural integrity.

I prefer blocks that are anywhere from eight to twelve inches thick. These should be rectangular in shape but will ultimately become a seven-sided figure. First, shave the top end at an angle of forty-five degrees. Then, starting at the middle of the opposite end, shave a right angle.

The A-frame trench is typically made for no more than two inhabitants. The following illustration details how a shelf can be cut into the side of your trench to support your blocks. (Blocks can also be staggered to create added support.) Once you have constructed the trench, throw some loose snow over the top to cover any holes. This shelter helps avoid dripping because of the sloped interior.

BENEFITS AND DRAWBACKS

Benefits
- ▲ Constructed entirely of snow.
- ▲ Angled interior is less prone to dripping than those of other shelters.
- ▲ Efficient use of snow. Blocks that are quarried to create your trench are then used to build an angled interior.

Drawbacks
- ▲ Cutting roof blocks to the proper dimensions can be challenging.

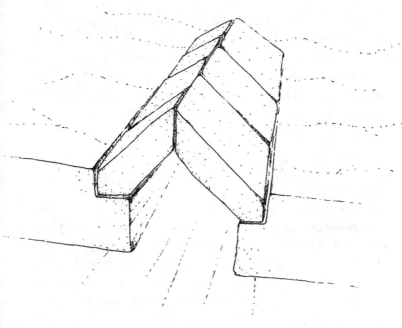

The A-frame trench.

Luxuries and Long-Term Considerations

The survivalist can get away with relatively little in the short term, but this doesn't mean that you shouldn't strive for comfort. Comfort means warmth and the potential for a better night's sleep. Survival isn't about enduring pain so much as learning to meet your needs through an awareness of, and appreciation for, available resources. Below are some options that can make your snow shelter even more inhabitable. A representation of all these considerations appears earlier in the chapter.

Elevated Sleeping Platforms

Warm air rises and cold air sinks. A raised bed with a cold sink—an area within the shelter that is lower than the sleeping platform—allows the camper to rest and sleep in the warmest part of the shelter. Whenever possible, doorways should be constructed at a level such that you crawl up and into the warmer interior of the shelter. This platform should be wide enough to accommodate your body as well as any natural insulation you use to create a buffer against the walls of your shelter.

Entrance Alcove and Extra Rooms

Having a large alcove—a covered space over your door—will protect your entryway from falling or drifting snow. It also allows you to place a layer of brush on the ground that you can crawl on as you get into and out of your shelter (which is preferable to crawling on snow). Rooms can be added to your shelter as time, energy, resources, and the desire for luxury allow.

One extra room that can prove invaluable is a lavatory. Because of the impracticality of opening and closing your door multiple times a night to go to the bathroom, having a designated space to urinate is a borderline necessity. (Bowels, of course, should always be emptied outside your shelter.)

Bedding and Insulation

If you can, build a buffer of space around your bed so that you and your sleeping bag don't brush up against the walls and gather moisture. An insulated bed is much more than a few sticks to help keep you off the ground. It traps your body heat and creates a comfortable place to sleep.

First, construct a frame of dead logs to contain your bedding. Your first layer should have enough mass to keep your later, finer materials from contacting the snow. Examples of this include hemlock boughs, spruce branches, and Japanese knotweed. The latter is an invasive plant species, so feel free to harvest this generously. Next, add choice bedding such as grasses, sedges, leaves, or cattails. This layer of insulating debris should be at least eight inches thick once it is compressed.

Beyond the bed, the survivalist can use any and all available insulating materials to stuff his or her shelter, much like a squirrel would use in creating a nest. Without a blanket or a sleeping bag, this debris keeps the inhabitant warm. When time and resources have enabled me to collect ample insulating material, I have been warm and comfortable. To implement a general insulating strategy, an oversized space is ideal with at least twenty-four inches of insulating debris cocooning your body.

Implementing these techniques will take you from merely surviving to finding true comfort. And in the long run this extra work will save you energy.

What to Do When There Is Little or No Snow

There will be times when you're faced with the contradiction of freezing temperatures but no available snow. In such cases, you will need to draw on all available resources, no matter how meager. During milder winters, snow accumulation is often fleeting or nonexistent. For what to do when there is no snow to keep you warm (an oxymoron if ever there was one), we'll now turn to debris and natural insulation and the ways you can use fire to add warmth.

The Debris Hut

The debris hut is a simple but effective shelter comprising heaps of natural debris, such as dead leaves and grasses, on a frame. The frame should be snug for the inhabitant, its compact size ensuring that your body effectively maintains warmth. I tend to rest on my side and build my frames a bit wider to accommodate my sleeping style. Another option is to build the frame oversized to the point that, once it is covered with two to four feet of debris, the inside can be stuffed with insulating material and used as a leaf crib.

▼▼▼

The following ideas can and should be integrated into any of the preceding shelter plans whenever possible. This will help create a place of great comfort and warmth. Without access to a sleeping bag or blanket, natural insulation should always be used.

A few things to keep in mind:

- Don't skimp on debris. A two-foot minimum thickness is standard for temperatures above freezing. When you get below the freezing mark, I would encourage a minimum of three feet. When you get below zero, aim for four feet.
- Close the door! Failing to close your door is like forgetting to secure the lid on a vacuum flask. What was once warm will quickly cool as energy is lost to the surrounding environment.
- Once your hut is complete, cover your debris with a loose layer of branches, but don't use anything heavy. Ideally, you want your lattice to keep any insulation from blowing away.
- One way to insulate yourself from the ground and create a comfortable bed is to stuff your shelter with debris. If you have a choice, dry grasses and leaves work best. Crawl inside and compress your insulation, adding more debris and compressing again. Once finished, you should have a minimum six-inch layer of compressed material.
- Your shelter will need upkeep. Over time, your walls will settle and become less airy. Be prepared to add more debris.

BENEFITS AND DRAWBACKS

Benefits
- No tools required
- Makes use of natural insulation
- Easily adapted to fit your needs

Drawbacks
- Ineffective when using damp or frozen leaf litter

Debris hut frame.

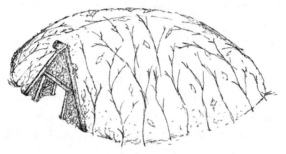

**Dead leaves and grasses are used in
the construction of the debris hut.**

The Leaf Crib

Imagine burrowing into a large pile of hay or leaves. Like our rodent kin who use nests to stay warm, we too can benefit from creating large piles of dry vegetation and crawling inside. The basic premise of the leaf crib is that of a container to hold natural insulation. Envision a corral made with stacked logs or, where snow cover dominates the landscape, blocks of snow. Leaves, grasses, sedges, and other natural materials are heaped into this space with the idea that, when finished, you will have an area to crawl into that will trap your body's heat.

It is important to note that simply curling up inside a pile of leaves is not sufficient—all of your insulation needs to be contained within either a shelter or a crib. If you were to create a vegetative pile in which to burrow, but it was not corralled in some fashion, you would soon find yourself cold and your pile spread out as you shifted throughout the night. Placing your insulation within walls will keep it where you need it most.

Walls or a container can be made in a variety of ways. Use the landscape to your advantage. Root balls can often be assimilated into your shelter plan. In areas where logs and dead trees are available, a cabin-style frame can easily be constructed. When I was leading an early spring outing in the Adirondacks with a group of young people, we once found ourselves in an area populated with boulders. Students integrated leaf cribs into naturally occurring containers (pockets in the landscape) to great success.

When constructing a container, it is important to keep in mind that it needs to be several feet longer and wider than the inhabitant and three to four feet deep. The interior of your crib should be large enough that your body is no farther than eighteen inches from each wall's edge. If you are sleeping under a clear sky, an unroofed crib may be enough. In rainy or snowy conditions, however, a brush- or bark-covered A-frame- or lean-to-style roof must be included. With the addition of a proper roof, the leaf crib can take more time to build than other shelters. Once it is constructed, however, you will be protected from the elements.

Being surrounded by insulation is one of the leaf crib's greatest benefits. Even if a shelter is properly constructed, I sometimes have trouble sleeping without the warmth and weight of a blanket. The leaf crib eliminates this problem. For the leaf crib to work, your materials ideally will be dry and in abundance. The leaf crib lends itself to creativity—don't hesitate to experiment.

The leaf crib can be easily assimilated into any snow shelter, making for decidedly more comfortable accommodations. One way to do this is to simply fill your shelter with insulation and burrow inside when it's time to go to sleep. Be mindful of trying not to shift your position in the night so you don't migrate from the center of your cocoon toward the walls.

To avoid coming into contact with the walls, you can go a step further and build a true container (sticks driven vertically into the ground) within your snow shelter. Your shelter, of course, must be large enough to accommodate these extra materials.

In many winter situations, locating adequate materials for the leaf crib simply isn't possible. Even in ideal settings, materials may be wet or

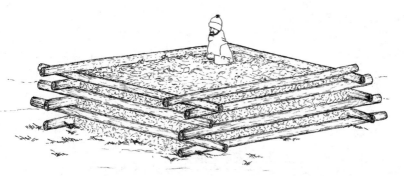

**Where snow is abundant, blocks can be used as a substitute
for logs in the construction of the leaf crib.**

inaccessible. To combat this issue, scour the landscape for suitable bedding
and *then* build your shelter (as opposed to the other way around).

I have built some of my most successful winter shelters in transition
areas, where two or more habitats collide (for more about transition
areas, see chapter 5). This enables you to take advantage of a multitude
of resources. One of my most memorable winter outings, in fact, involved
the use of sedges to insulate a two-person snow trench, which allowed for
an excellent night's sleep.

BENEFITS AND DRAWBACKS

Benefits
- ▲ No tools required
- ▲ Makes use of natural insulation
- ▲ Can be integrated into any existing shelter plan

Drawbacks
- ▲ A roof is a must if precipitation is expected, and constructing it
  consumes time and energy.
- ▲ A crib is ineffective when you use damp or frozen leaf litter.

▼▼▼

Creating Warmth

One of the most challenging cold-weather situations occurs when snow is absent but leaf litter is damp or frozen. This is a time when the benefit of shelter is not enough to maintain your core temperature. In these instances, you must learn how to manipulate fire to meet your needs.

The Lean-to with Reflector Wall

Much of the heat from an outdoor fire is lost to the atmosphere. When I've needed fire instead of shelter to maintain warmth, if I don't have the time or resources to improve the efficiency of my setup I've found that I burn as much wood in one night as I do in a week in my home. Fire is indispensable, but it takes a great deal of wood to keep a group warm for the night. On this note, I would encourage you to build a lean-to with a reflector wall.

Your lean-to should be five to six feet tall with a roof pitched at an angle of about fifty degrees. Make this large enough to suit your needs but no larger. Be sure to build your lean-to with a healthy supply of sturdy beams. These beams not only will support outside thatching or bark but will also absorb heat. Sheath your roof with bark, grasses, or other materials. This will reflect the fire's heat and protect you from wind and precipitation. Close in both sides of your lean-to such that it will further contain heat and eliminate drafts.

A lean-to coupled with a reflector wall will maximize your fire's heating potential. The reflector itself can be almost anything—a stack of logs, a root ball, a boulder, a snowbank, or even another lean-to. Regardless of what you choose, make sure that it's positioned far enough from your flame that it doesn't run the risk of catching on fire. If you are using a snow bench as a reflector, be sure to cover it with brush, bark, or some type of insulation so you can sit down without getting damp. With the addition of fire, three or four lean-tos (facing one other) are as effective as an enclosed shelter. This is worth the effort, as it does a magnificent job of containing warmth.

The lean-to is most effective when paired with a reflective device.

When using an open-faced lean-to in conjunction with a reflector wall, make your fire wide enough (roughly the length of your person) so it will heat the entirety of your body when you're lying down. Regardless of the arrangement, be sure to create a suitable bed that is positioned against the back wall of your structure. You can craft either an insulated bed (to keep you off the ground) or an elevated platform (this will enable any heat from the fire to radiate beneath you).

Hot Rocks

Nonsedimentary and nonglassy rocks (granite being ideal) can be heated in the fire and used as body warmers or heaters in non-brush-covered shelters. It is important to note that if you are not sure if a rock will explode, you should distance yourself from the fire. Using heated rocks is an age-old technology. Rocks can also be placed in improvised vessels (a hollowed pumpkin, for example) to boil water.

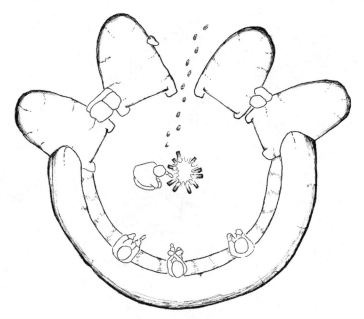

**Snow walls can serve the dual purpose
of wind break and fire reflector.**

During an Adirondack survival outing, one of my students became ill with fever. The only way to warm her was to give her a heated rock. We wrapped this warm (but not too warm) rock in a T-shirt, which she then held to her body. She recovered to the point that we successfully hiked out with her the next morning.

What to Do above Timberline

If you find yourself above timberline, you will be without certain resources. There is no need to panic. In such cases, simply create a snow cave, snow trench, or block shelter and insulate yourself from the ground as best you can. This is a short-term solution, but it will get you through the night. If you find yourself with little snow or other resources, you may need to change your elevation by moving downward to find what you need. Mountaineering comes with its own unique risks and challenges; I would recommend traveling with an experienced guide when venturing into extreme environments.

Exercises

1. Construct one of the aforementioned shelters, incorporating the following luxuries into your design: an entrance alcove and extra rooms, a double-blocked door, and an elevated sleeping platform. Challenge yourself by using improvised tools to move, excavate, or quarry snow.

2. Experiment with different ways of maintaining warmth overnight without the aid of a sleeping bag, such as building a leaf crib, stuffing your clothing with natural insulation, building a fire with a reflector wall, or using heated rocks. As a precaution, make sure you have an effective backup plan.

3. Build the same shelter in different locations using different snow types. Note the benefits and drawbacks of each. Does direct sunlight cause your shelter to melt or sag? Are higher elevations and open areas more prone to wind chill? Are the types of wood and plant material at your disposal suitable for shelter construction?

▲▲▲▲

Chapter 4

Water

We had been saving our thirst for a long time.
Now knee-deep by the holes in the clay bottom, we cupped
our hands and started drinking out of the river.

Norman Maclean, *A River Runs Through It*

Several years ago I dragged my sons, Jacob and Aron, with me on a camping trip into the Catskill Mountains. This particular winter was virtually snowless in our part of the state, so we were excited to find a good covering when we entered the mountain region.

Our plan was to sleep in our van and hike Slide Mountain the next day. We arrived at our destination earlier than we had anticipated, so we decided to go on a hike to kill some time. After twenty minutes I ventured from the trail to inspect some nearby cliffs. My curiosity led me to a natural spring that was gushing from the bottom of a small ledge.

What made this such an amazing find? Where the spring emerged from the hillside was a small cave where, if need be, a suitable shelter could have been made for two or three people. Shelter and water all in one! We could have stayed there for weeks! We all drank from this wonderful source. Despite temperatures in the single digits, this spring was flowing freely.

It's difficult to describe how I feel when I find a new spring. It adds to my sense of belonging and connection with the outdoors. I've always enjoyed bringing youth groups to natural springs. For many of my participants, this is the first time they've sipped water directly from the earth. I view it as a rite of passage, much like a graduation ceremony.

Hydration

Once you've identified a means of maintaining your core temperature, hydration is next on your list of concerns. Without water the human body can survive only a few days. After three days, particularly under extreme duress, you will die without adequate hydration.

Rick Curtis, Director of Princeton University's Outdoor Action Program, recommends drinking a minimum of four quarts of water a day when hiking during the winter. Much of the survivalist's hydration, in fact, is lost through respiration. Not only are humidity levels lower at this time of the year, but cold air is heated in the lungs and then exhaled saturated with moisture.[1]

The easiest way to tell whether you're adequately hydrated is to monitor the color of your urine. You should be voiding your bladder at regular intervals, and your urine should be light yellow to clear. There are a number of consequences if you become dehydrated. According to the Mayo Clinic, mild to moderate dehydration is likely to cause

- Dry, sticky mouth
- Sleepiness or tiredness—children are likely to be less active than usual
- Thirst
- Decreased urine output
- Few or no tears when crying
- Dry skin
- Headache
- Constipation
- Dizziness or lightheadedness

Severe dehydration, which is a medical emergency, may cause:

- Extreme thirst
- Extreme fussiness or sleepiness in infants and children; irritability and confusion in adults

- Dry mouth, skin, and mucous membranes
- Absence of sweat
- Little or no urination (any urine produced will be dark yellow or amber)
- Sunken eyes
- Shriveled and dry skin that lacks elasticity and doesn't "bounce back" when pinched
- In infants, sunken fontanels—the soft spots on the top of a baby's head
- Low blood pressure
- Rapid heartbeat
- Rapid breathing
- No tears when crying
- Fever
- In the most serious cases, delirium or unconsciousness[2]

In addition to making sure that you get enough to drink, you need to be aware that ingesting cold water robs your body of calories. (The body expends energy melting snow and ice as well.) Drinking cold water and eating clean snow are fine if you have a surplus of energy-rich foods and you're only out hiking for the day. It is an altogether different matter, however, if you're attempting to subsist on limited calories. In addition to the need to boil water to ensure it is safe to drink, is also important that even water deemed safe be heated to at least body temperature.

Purification

Water found in streams, creeks, ponds, and lakes may contain viruses and bacteria that can induce illness. It is for this reason that water obtained from these sources should always be purified before consumption. Keep in mind, however, that these processes will not remove chemical toxins.

Boiling Water

When in doubt, boil your water. If you don't have a metal pot or cup in which to boil, there are two types of containers that are applicable to a survival situation: coal-burned bowls and white pine bark containers. Both of these are to be used in conjunction with rock boiling, a process whereby hot rocks are dropped in water or snow. (For information on heating rocks, see chapter 3.) Information on how to fashion these traditional vessels is detailed in chapter 6.

I prefer rocks that range in size from a golf ball to a baseball depending on the breadth of my container. When effectively heated, these stones will be glowing red. They can then be removed with sticks or tongs and placed in your container of water or snow to boil. Multiple rocks may be required. I always like to have a few extras waiting for me in the fire should I need them.

If rocks are hard to come by, it's possible to use a pine bark container over a bed of coals. I like to buffer my container by placing green sticks roughly one inch in diameter over the coals. Your container won't last as long if you use it in this way, but it will bring water to a boil. I have also used pine bark containers to melt snow by placing them near the fire. This process takes considerably longer but will prolong the life of your container and eventually bring your water to body temperature.

How long should you boil your water? Citing the Wilderness Medical Society, Rick Curtis recommends the following: "Water temperatures above 160° Fahrenheit kill all pathogens within 30 minutes. Water temperatures above 185° Fahrenheit kill all pathogens within a few minutes."[3] By the time your water reaches a rolling boil, it's safe to drink, even at high altitudes. (Water will actually boil at a temperature lower than 212 degrees Fahrenheit at any altitude above sea level. This is because air pressure decreases as altitude increases.) If possible, you should also filter cloudy water through a cloth or grass nest to remove any sediment beforehand.

▼▼▼

Modern Techniques

The general consensus with regard to the use of modern purification techniques such as filters and chlorine or iodine tablets is that they are less effective than boiling or shouldn't be used at all. When it comes to pump filters, the risk is that any water remaining in your pump will freeze, compromising the seals and possibly cracking the unit, rendering it useless. When you use chemical treatments such as iodine, your water should be over sixty-eight degrees Fahrenheit, as these are ineffective at low temperatures.[4]

If you wanted to use a liquid-based treatment, you would not only have to ensure that your water was at minimum of sixty-eight degrees but also have to keep your purifier from freezing by placing it against your body or in an inside pocket of your jacket. As an experiment, I once tested some of my chlorine-based drops outside to see if they would freeze. They most surely did. This makes the use of fire a virtual necessity during the winter.

Procuring Water

Now I'll turn my attention to the various means of procuring water—snow and ice accumulation, natural springs, and trees.

Snow and Ice

Snow and ice are advantageous to hydration because they're easy to collect. Still, they will need to be not only melted but heated up to at least body temperature. Snow, assuming it is not discolored, is to be considered a safe source of water and need not be boiled. Snow is mostly air, which accounts for its wonderful insulating properties. This also means, however, that it will take a great deal of snow to obtain significant quantities of drinkable water.

Ice is only as pure as its source. The risk with ice is that if it's gathered from a body of water that contains viruses or bacteria, these may harm you if your water isn't boiled. If there's any question as to the purity of your source, it's best to bring your water to a boil. Look for sources that are clean and free of debris. The process of melting snow and ice can be expedited if there's already water in your container.

Natural Springs

A spring is a place where groundwater comes out of the earth. Natural springs are generally safe for drinking, but you should carefully consider whether they are the best option. Beyond wanting to heat your water to help with caloric considerations, it is good to think about the circumstances under which you find your spring. Could it be polluted by industry or agriculture? Is it flowing or is it stagnant? Has it been tainted with animal waste? A colleague of mine once drank from a natural spring only to realize afterward that it contained a decaying frog.

The best way to find a spring is to move upstream from a small creek or other drainage. This can be especially fruitful in hilly or mountainous areas. Look for smaller tributaries. Often your water will be fed by precipitation. If you're lucky, though, you'll find a spot where water is literally flowing out of the ground. Look for wet areas where snow can't accumulate. Springs can be cleaned of debris, made deeper, and left to settle before you draw from them.

I have found dozens of springs near my home. I often locate signs of old farmsteads (stone foundations, for example), indicating the judicious choice of early settlers to have a safe and steady supply of water. When I'm camping and hiking I often secure all my water from natural springs. Keep in mind that spring water is warmer than running water found in creeks or streams. Spring water comes out of the ground at a constant temperature relative to the earth. If you are unable to heat your water, springs may be a good alternative because they not only are generally free of bacteria but include the added benefit of requiring fewer calories to digest.

When it comes to obvious sources of water such as creeks, streams, brooks, and rivers, it is best practice to assume these are polluted. Unlike springs, obvious sources of water are likely to be full of impurities and will need to be boiled.

Trees

In New York State the tree-tapping season has changed greatly over the last decade. This seems to be a reflection of global climate trends and winters that are far less predictable than in years past. Traditionally, maple sugaring season has been held in late winter or early spring (March). Ideal conditions for sugaring come when nighttime temperatures are below freezing and daytime temperatures are above the freezing mark. With this in mind, it is important to consider trees a potential source of water.

Trees that can be tapped to collect sap and consumed without treatment include maples, birches, walnuts, hickories, and sycamores. These all have trace amounts of sugar in their sap, so in addition to tasting sweet their water will provide a boost in energy. To tap a tree without a drill and spile, I like to bore a hole on the underside of a horizontal branch with a knife or stone. If conditions are right and your hole is deep enough, sap will begin to drip into your container.

▲▲▲▲

83

Exercises

1. Practice boiling water using hot rocks in a pine bark container or coal-burned bowl. Note how many rocks it takes for the water to reach a rolling boil, as well as how long it takes for it to reach a comfortable drinking temperature. To make your water more vitamin-rich, experiment using pine needles (see chapter 5) to brew tea.

2. Spend a day outside when you know conditions are conducive to tapping. Experiment with collecting sap from the deciduous trees listed above, noting the ease with which each produces sap. Collect the sap in a container of your own design and without the aid of a spile.

3. Take a hike through unfamiliar terrain with the intention of locating a water source. Note what changes in the landscape or environment might alert you to the presence of water. Can you hear a stream rushing in the distance? Is erosion present in the form of a ravine, gorge, or valley? Is there a greater presence of wildlife in one area than in others? As an added challenge, search for a natural spring by following a stream, brook, or creek to a higher elevation.

Chapter 5

Sustenance

He took out his knife, opened it and stuck it in the log.
Then he pulled up the sack, reached into it and
brought out one of the trout. . . . They were both males;
long gray-white strips of milt, smooth and clean.

Ernest Hemingway, *Big Two-Hearted River*

Years ago I led a survival excursion on my property in upstate New York. Aside from the goal of building shelters and drinking water from a natural spring, I wanted the group to forage for food. Although this wasn't a congregation of experienced young people, under the tutelage of knowledgeable adults they fared well and even had enough for leftovers.

I have since procured many meals from the wild, feasting on nature's bounty. I have even supplemented meals at home with foraged edibles. Most of these experiences have taken place during times of plenty, between early spring and the first snowfall.

Foraging in the winter is a much more difficult task, but with practice you can identify wild edible plants and trap animals. It would be misleading, of course, to suggest that food procured during the winter compares to the array of edibles that exist during the warmer months. In many habitats, not only will the meager rations that can be found be far from tasty, but calories will be limited.

In my home state of New York, a locale with a great variety of habitats, winter foraging can vary from abundant to scarce. The 6.1 million acres comprising Adirondack Park, for example, are a much more challenging place to find edibles (let alone winter edibles) in comparison with the more temperate Finger Lakes region. In fact, the word "Adirondack" roughly translates to "bark eater," a Mohican word reflecting the limited availability of food.

Our ancestors who made their home in the northern regions survived the winters by collecting and preparing food for storage and stockpiling larders. They did this well in advance of the arrival of cold temperatures when bounties from the growing season were abundant. In general, winters were a time for reflection, storytelling, and crafting. Tools and other useful items were built and repaired during this time, as most food was safely stowed and available for consumption.

There was always the anticipation of upcoming needs and challenges. Winter was a time when nets could be crafted before the spring salmon run. Stone bowls, which required repetitive motions to produce, were fashioned during the colder months while people sat in a lodge near the fire, listening to the stories of elders. Without question, people of the past hunted and trapped in the winter months but not with an air of panic or urgency. Hunting was in the hands of masters, who knew that fresh meat would be a welcome addition to the stew pot and would help extend stored rations.

If you contrast this traditional strategy for meeting the caloric needs of a large group of people with what a modern person thrust into a survival experience is likely to encounter, you will discover a significant challenge that is not to be underestimated. When the difficulty of hunting is coupled with other challenges that the unprepared winter survivalist is likely to face, the result will be a profound caloric deficit. The ability to procure enough food each day within the context of a winter survival situation and to emerge well nourished is something that can be mastered only over time. As I've become a more proficient winter forager and primitive trapper, my confidence has grown. I have come closer to the eventual goal of starting with nothing and meeting my long-term needs.

The best advice I can offer is to start learning about plants—not tomorrow but today. View them not only as a source of food but also as potential medicine and crafting materials. This will help train your eyes to see in a new way. Integrate wild edibles and useful plants into your life so they become part of your routine. Learning plant identification takes time, and there are no shortcuts to becoming confident in your abilities. Knowing plants and becoming familiar with the unique challenges of winter foraging are skills that are best tackled one step at a time.

Practicing in a controlled setting will help you appreciate the notion of risk versus reward. Foraging, hunting, and trapping all require time and energy. The more experienced you are with these skills, the better you'll be at judging when and where they should be employed. And by doing so, you'll use your time and energy to the best of your ability. With patience and practice, your effort will be rewarded. If this important skill is neglected, however, the outcome of a long-term survival situation will likely be dire.

As Sam Thayer states in *Nature's Garden*, "In a short-term survival situation, food is of minor importance. However, in long-term survival . . . it is of paramount importance."[1] In a situation where you are truly lost or stranded, it may become necessary to eat, trap, and hunt anything you can find. It is important, however, to keep the idea of stewardship in mind when attempting to master these skills. Taking from nature is something we do every day. The problem is that most of us are disengaged from this process and fail to see how our actions impact the environment. By practicing primitive skills, you can directly see the result of your dependence on the land and the animals that inhabit it.

For more than fifteen years I've been venturing into the same forested area behind the school where I work. These woods have supplied us with shelter, fire, crafting materials, and wild edibles. I'm proud to say that this habitat remains a vital home to a great variety of wildlife. Despite our presence, I have even noticed an increase in the prevalence of certain species of plants.

Almost every year we have harvested a basswood tree, as it is renowned as a source of fibrous material. The spring bark is stripped and rolled into coils. These coils are then submerged in a pond and left for several weeks. This retting process, also known as "controlled rotting," helps to separate the layers of inner bark, which are then twisted into all thicknesses and lengths of cordage.

The hunt for the proper tree can sometimes take as long as the harvest itself. Each tree is scrutinized not only to guarantee quality bark but to ensure that what we select will leave the forest a more vibrant place. Proper gathering is much like gardening—when forests are thinned, it leaves room for those plants that remain to proliferate. Keep the following in mind when gathering wild plants, and in a true time of need, take what you have to. Give thanks with the intention of returning to care for this or another place in the future.

Here are some important things to keep in mind when foraging:

- Keep an eye out for plants that are rare or limited and let these plants be.
- Gather only what you will use.
- Minimize your environmental impact. Maintain a healthy relationship with the habitat from which you have gathered.
- If you are not 100 percent certain of a plant's identity, don't eat it.

Plants: Edible, Medicinal—and They Don't Run!

Below is a list of plants that are available during the winter months. It is important to note that this book is not a plant identification guide. I suggest creating your own list for your region and any areas you plan to visit. Get to know these plants and refer to the books listed. Remember that 100 percent certainty is critical when consuming wild edibles.

The following list is by no means comprehensive. There are plants that are available during the winter that I have not included. Arrowhead, for example, has edible roots. I have decided to omit this because it is found underwater. If not already covered in ice, it will be dangerous to gather and not worth the risk.

Other plants I have excluded from this list may have limited value or are scarce because their aboveground appearance provides little to no indication of their bounty. I have, however, included plants that offer crafting materials or have medicinal value. It will ultimately be your responsibility to become familiar with the plants available in your area and anywhere you travel.

The winter forager faces obstacles that are not an issue during more temperate months. Frozen ground, snow cover, and a lack of identifiable traits (leaves, for example) are but a few of these challenges. The winter forager may have to access a shovel, digging stick, or fire to extract root crops or tubers.

I recommend learning plants during all times of the year, looking to discover not only edible plants but utilitarian and medicinal plants as well. Although I have chosen to include plants that are more abundant during the winter, the more you know the better off you'll be. It's even possible to find plants out of season. One example of this is the dandelion—remarkably, I have found dandelion flowers every month of the year. Microclimates enable certain plants to thrive despite the season.

During the New Year's holiday one year my wife and I decided to stay in the Catskill Mountains. This particular winter was without snow, and we were surprised to find a bumper crop of beechnuts when we went out for a hike. I felt like an opportunistic squirrel as I gathered my bounty. In the Northeast, beechnuts are not considered a winter edible, but there we were, collecting at will. The best advice I can offer to any forager is keep your eyes open and expect the unexpected.

A Field Guide to Edible Wild Plants: Eastern and Central North America (The Peterson Field Guide Series) includes useful information on finding edible plants within the different habitats that exist in North America. Not only are the edibles that are likely to be found in each habitat listed, but each is broken down by season so you can focus on those plants that are of value for a given time of year. For tree identification, I recommend *A Field Guide to Trees and Shrubs: Northeastern and North-central United States and Southeastern and South-central Canada (The Peterson Field Guide Series)*.

The following plants appear in alphabetical order and were selected based on availability, ease of identification, and their medicinal and utilitarian properties.

Aspen, Bigtooth *(Populus grandidentata)*
Aspen, Quaking *(Populus tremuloides)*

- ▲ DESCRIPTION: Aspens can grow upwards of eighty feet. The bark is smooth, pale, and olive in color.
- ▲ HABITAT: They prefer forest edges and well-drained soil.
- ▲ RANGE: They can be found in southern Canada and the northern third of the United States, following the Rocky Mountains southward.
- ▲ FOOD: The inner bark, although often bitter, is fit for consumption.
- ▲ MEDICINE: Aspens contain resinous buds that can be used as an antiseptic. The inner bark or leaves may be steeped in water for a pain-relieving tea.[2]
- ▲ UTILITY:
  - ▲ Members of the poplar family provide excellent materials for friction kits. These trees are also a wonderful choice for coal burning.

Birches *(Betula)*

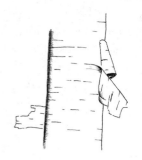

- ▲ DESCRIPTION: Birches are medium-sized trees of the North Country. Depending on the species, bark color can range from white to dark brown. The bark has horizontal scars.
- ▲ HABITAT: Birches can inhabit a variety of habitats (depending on the species) including mature forests, damp areas, and alpine areas.

- ▲ **RANGE:** They are found across the globe but prefer northern environments.
- ▲ **FOOD:** The dried and ground inner bark has been used historically as coarse flour.
- ▲ **MEDICINE:** Tea made from bark and twigs may alleviate fever and mild pain.[3]
- ▲ **UTILITY:**
  - ▲ If conditions are favorable—that is, day temperatures are well above freezing and night temperatures are below freezing—birches are an excellent source of water. Sap can be boiled to make syrup.
  - ▲ Birch bark—especially that of the paper birch—makes an excellent fire starter.
  - ▲ In early spring, when the sap is flowing, sheets of bark can be removed and used in a variety of ways, including shelter covering and folded baskets.
  - ▲ Birches make excellent firewood.
  - ▲ Birch twigs, made flexible by twisting, can be used as a binding.

▲▲▲▲

91

Burdock *(Arctium lappa)*

- ▲ **DESCRIPTION:** Burdock is a biennial that grows as high as five feet. The winter burdock is easily identified by its dried, skeletal appearance.
- ▲ **HABITAT:** It prefers fields, disturbed areas, and the edges of forests and requires direct sunlight to proliferate.
- ▲ **RANGE:** It is found throughout Canada and the United States (with the exception of the extreme Southwest).

- ▲ FOOD: The dead stalks of second-year growth may indicate valuable roots from earlier growth.[4]
- ▲ UTILITY:
  - ▲ The dried stalk can be used as a spindle for friction fire kits.
  - ▲ The burs can be used as Velcro.

Cattails *(Typha)*

- ▲ DESCRIPTION: The cattail is renowned for its utility and the sustenance it offers throughout the year. It is best identified via its proximity to water and the fibrous, fluffy appearance of the head (which resembles a hot dog in the summer).
- ▲ HABITAT: The cattail is found in or near quiet, shallow waters such as ponds, lake edges, and marshes.
- ▲ RANGE: It is prevalent throughout North America.
- ▲ FOOD: Cattail tubers can be unearthed and boiled much like potatoes. From late winter to early spring, it is possible to find shoots emerging from the base of the plant.[5]
- ▲ UTILITY:
  - ▲ The dried, fluffy seed heads make excellent coal extenders. This material does not ignite on its own, but will "grab a coal" and enable it to expand. Other flammable materials can be added to your cattail tinder to help it ignite. The seed heads also make wonderful insulation.
  - ▲ Dried leaves can be used for a multitude of purposes, including bedding, insulation, and thatching for shelters.
  - ▲ The inner stalk of the cattail can be used as a hand drill material and for arrow shafts.

▼▼▼

Cedar, Northern White *(Thuja occidentalis)*

- ▲ DESCRIPTION: Cedars are medium-sized trees that can grow twenty-five to fifty feet in height. They have small, erect oblong cones and scale-like leaves.
- ▲ HABITAT: They prefer moist, boggy areas but can also be found in drier conditions.
- ▲ RANGE: Cedars are commonly found throughout the North.
- ▲ FOOD: The leaves and young shoots are edible and can be made into tea.[6]
- ▲ UTILITY:
  - ▲ Cedar offers excellent materials for friction fire kits.
  - ▲ The inner bark makes excellent medium-strength cordage and a superior tinder bundle.
  - ▲ Boughs can be used for bedding and signal fires.

▲▲▲▲

93

Cottonwood, Common *(Populus deltoides)*

- ▲ DESCRIPTION: The cottonwood is a large tree of bottomlands. Mature trees are distinguished in the winter by their rough bark. (Younger trees have light green bark.)
- ▲ HABITAT: Cottonwoods prefer the moisture of bottomlands, rivers, and lakesides.
- ▲ RANGE: They are found throughout Canada and the United States.
- ▲ FOOD: The cambium, or inner bark, can be harvested and eaten fresh or dried.[7]
- ▲ UTILITY:
  - ▲ Cottonwood makes an excellent wood for friction fire kits.
  - ▲ The inner bark can be used for tinder as well as rough cordage.

Dogbane *(Apocynum)*

- ▲ DESCRIPTION: Dogbane is a branching perennial and a member of the milkweed family.
- ▲ HABITAT: It is often found in open fields.
- ▲ RANGE: It is found throughout the United States and north to British Columbia.
- ▲ FOOD: Dogbane offers no nutritional benefits and in fact can be poisonous.[8]
- ▲ UTILITY:
  - ▲ The dried stalks can be harvested for cordage. Look for plants that lack dark areas, which is indicative of rot.
  - ▲ The inner ovum of the seed pods can be used as a coal extender.

Fir, Balsam *(Abies balsamea)*

- ▲ DESCRIPTION: Balsam firs are pointed evergreens. Their needles range from three-eighths inch to one and a quarter inches long with two whitish lines on the underside and erect one- to three-inch cones. The bark is smooth with many resin-containing blisters.
- ▲ HABITAT: Balsam firs thrive in cool, damp woodlands and higher elevations.
- ▲ RANGE: They are native to most of eastern and central Canada as well as the northeastern United States.
- ▲ FOOD: The balsam fir can be used for emergency food. The pitch contained within the blisters can be eaten. The inner bark can be dried and ground into flour.

- ▲ MEDICINE: The resin from balsam can be used as an antiseptic for cuts and burns.[9]
- ▲ UTILITY:
  - ▲ Glue or adhesive can be fashioned from balsam pitch.
  - ▲ Signal fires can be made using balsam firs (and any other evergreens), and boughs can be used as bedding.

Garlic Mustard (*Alliaria petiolata*)

- ▲ DESCRIPTION: Mustards are best recognized in winter by the remains of the ascending seed pods found on the dried stalk. This is a variable group of plants.
- ▲ HABITAT: Mustards prefer forest edges, fields, and waste ground.
- ▲ RANGE: They are found throughout most of the United States and Canada.
- ▲ FOOD: Because these plants photosynthesize throughout the winter, the leaves are available for consumption.[10]
- ▲ UTILITY:
  - ▲ The dried stalks of mustards make excellent fire-starting material.

▲▲▲▲

95

Hackberry, American (*Celtis occidentalis*)

- ▲ DESCRIPTION: This deciduous tree is most easily identified in the winter by its distinctive gray, corky bark marked by irregularly spaced ridges with flat, smooth spaces in between.
- ▲ HABITAT: It is found in a variety of

woodland habitats, but prefers the edges of forests.

- ▲ RANGE: The American hackberry ranges from southern Ontario and Quebec to the central United States.
- ▲ FOOD: It bears small, dark fruit that can be found from fall through early winter.[11]

Hemlock, Eastern *(Tsuga canadensis)*

- ▲ DESCRIPTION: The eastern hemlock is a flat-needled evergreen. Its needles resemble those of balsam fir and are one-quarter to three-fourths inch in length. This tree can grow as tall as 150 feet and has an irregular, feathery outline.

- ▲ HABITAT: The eastern hemlock prefers wet, shady woodlands. This includes valleys as well as rocky woods.
- ▲ RANGE: It grows throughout the United States and Canada.
- ▲ FOOD: The tree's needles can be chopped and made into tea, and the dried inner bark can be made into flour. *Do not confuse eastern hemlock with poison hemlock, a branched biennial that is similar in appearance to Wild Carrot (Queen Anne's Lace).*[12]
- ▲ UTILITY:
  - ▲ Hemlock burns well and makes excellent coals.

Jerusalem Artichoke *(Helianthus tuberosus)*

- ▲ DESCRIPTION: The Jerusalem artichoke is best identified by its tall winter remains. Leaf scars or remaining leaves are arranged alternately up the stalk. Medium-sized tubers can be found under the earth. Soil generally determines the quality and quantity of this food source.

- ▲ HABITAT: It inhabits fields, forest edges, and waste ground.
- ▲ RANGE: This plant is found from Georgia north to Ontario and Saskatchewan.
- ▲ FOOD: The tubers can be eaten raw or cooked like potatoes. The Jerusalem artichoke is one of the best wild edibles.[13]

Labrador Tea *(Rhododendron groenlandicum)*

- ▲ DESCRIPTION: Labrador tea is a short evergreen North Country shrub. Its leaves are leathery and untoothed.
- ▲ HABITAT: It prefers peat soils and bogs.
- ▲ RANGE: It can be found in Canada and the northern United States.
- ▲ FOOD: Its leaves can be brewed into a mild tea.[14]

Maples *(Acer)*

- ▲ DESCRIPTION: This large group of trees is best identified by following the various species through their yearly life cycle.
- ▲ HABITAT: Maples grow in wet woods and rich soils.
- ▲ RANGE: They are found throughout the northern United States and Canada.
- ▲ FOOD: Their dried inner bark can be ground into flour. Some maples keep their seeds through the winter. These seeds can also be

dried and ground into flour or eaten raw.[15]

▲ UTILITY:

　▲ If conditions are favorable—that is, days are well above
　freezing and nights are below freezing—maples are
　an excellent source of water (sap). This can be boiled
　to make syrup.

　▲ Maple makes excellent firewood.

　▲ This hardwood can be used for
　bow construction.

Milkweed, Common *(Asclepias syriaca)*

▲ DESCRIPTION: The winter remains of the
milkweed can be identified by their fibrous
stalks and opened seed capsules.

▲ HABITAT: Milkweed grows in fields,
waste ground, and forest edges.

▲ RANGE: It is found in the northern
United States and Canada.

▲ FOOD: Milkweed offers no nutritional
benefits.[16]

▲ UTILITY:

　▲ Although not ideal during winter, this
　fibrous plant can be used for cordage. It can also be used
　as a tinder bundle additive. The milkweed ovum, which
　is found within the seed capsule, can be used as a coal
　extender or a spark catcher. I have used this amazing re-
　source successfully with a traditional flint and steel kit as
　well as a fire piston. (The fire piston is a device in which a
　smooth hardwood plunger is forced into a cylinder. This
　"piston" action heats the air inside to the point that it can
　bring tinder to a smolder.)

Mountain Ash *(Pyrus)*

- ▲ DESCRIPTION: Identification of this opposite-branching tree is aided by the presence of clusters of orange-colored fruit.
- ▲ HABITAT: It prefers moist, cool woodlands.
- ▲ RANGE: The mountain ash is found in southern Canada through the northern United States.
- ▲ FOOD: The fruit of the mountain ash becomes more palatable after repeated freezings. It can be cooked or eaten raw.[17]

Mullien, Common *(Verbascum thapsus)*

- ▲ DESCRIPTION: This biennial is a field plant best identified by its large seed head, which can grow up to six feet tall.
- ▲ HABITAT: Mullein prefers waste ground, disturbed areas, and fields.
- ▲ RANGE: This plant can be found throughout most of Canada and the United States.
- ▲ FOOD: Mullien offers no nutritional benefits.[18]
- ▲ UTILITY:
  - ▲ Mullein stalks (which are not cracked) can be used as hand drills.

▲▲▲▲
99

Oaks *(Quercus)*

- ▲ DESCRIPTION: Although leaves within the oak family are variable, all oaks can be recognized by roundish, capped nuts (acorns).

- ▲ HABITAT: Oaks inhabit upper woodlands, north- and east-facing hillsides, and well-drained soils.
- ▲ RANGE: Oaks are widespread but generally range east of the Mississippi in the United States to southern Canada.
- ▲ FOOD: These have acorns that last through the winter (in productive years acorns will be available until they sprout in the early spring). The acorns of all oaks are edible, although the nuts of red oaks are bitter. Crushed nuts require leaching or boiling to rid them of tannins.[19]
- ▲ UTILITY:
  - ▲ Oak makes excellent firewood.

Pines *(Pinus)*

- ▲ DESCRIPTION: Pines make up a large group of needled evergreens. The needles are grouped in bundles of two to five.
- ▲ HABITAT: Pines have varied habitats, from well-drained soils to moist areas.
- ▲ RANGE: They are found throughout the United States and Canada.
- ▲ FOOD: The needles of pines can be chopped and steeped in hot water to make tea. The inner bark is a valuable survival staple.
- ▲ MEDICINE: Pine needles are rich in Vitamin C.[20]
- ▲ UTILITY:
  - ▲ The bark of the white pine is an invaluable resource. Sheets of bark can be stripped from the branches of younger trees (sometimes requiring the heat of a fire) and folded into containers that can be used as water vessels and for rock boiling.
  - ▲ Pine boughs can be used for bedding and signal fires.

Reed *(Phragmites communis)*

- ▲ DESCRIPTION: Reed can be identified
  in the winter (where it is often found
  in large stands) by its feathery terminal
  flower cluster. This grass can grow up to
  fifteen feet in height.
- ▲ HABITAT: Reed enjoys moist areas, taking
  root in areas too dry for cattails.
- ▲ RANGE: It is found from Canada to Texas.
- ▲ FOOD: In the winter, flour can be
  obtained from the rootstock.[21]
- ▲ UTILITY:
  - ▲ The dried stalks can be used for a variety of purposes,
    including bedding, thatching, arrow shafts, and kindling.

Rock Tripe *(Umbilicaria and Gyrophora)*

- ▲ DESCRIPTION: Rock tripe is olive-gray in
  color and can grow up to eight inches in
  circumference. This lichen is brittle when
  dried and has a leathery feel when wet.
- ▲ HABITAT: It is found on rocks and
  rock faces.
- ▲ RANGE: It ranges from the Arctic through the mountains
  of Georgia.
- ▲ FOOD: Rock tripe should be boiled in several changes of water
  to remove bitterness. Eat a small amount at first to ensure that
  you don't have an adverse reaction.[22]

▼▼▼

Roses *(Rosa)*

- ▲ DESCRIPTION: Roses can be identified in the winter by their red fruits and thorns.
- ▲ HABITAT: Roses prefer fields, forest edges, and waste areas.
- ▲ RANGE: They are found throughout Canada and the United States.
- ▲ FOOD: The flesh of the rose hip (the fruit of the rose) is an excellent winter food source. Some varieties of rose have extremely large hips.
- ▲ MEDICINE: Because rose hips are high in Vitamin C, they help prevent scurvy.[23]
- ▲ UTILITY:
  - ▲ Stems that are straight and thick can be used for hand drills. They can also be used for basketry and arrow shafts.

Spruces *(Picea)*

- ▲ DESCRIPTION: Spruces are Christmas tree-shaped evergreens with sharp, pointed needles. Needles are arranged around the twigs.
- ▲ HABITAT: Spruces can be found in a variety of habitats, from well-drained forests to wet, boggy soil.
- ▲ RANGE: They are found from Canada through the northern United States.
- ▲ FOOD: Spruce needles can be boiled to make tea. The inner bark can be dried and ground into flour. The condensed sap can be chewed like gum.

- ▲ MEDICINE: Spruce pitch is an effective salve for treating wounds and cuts.[24]
- ▲ UTILITY:
  - ▲ Spruce boughs make a wonderful lattice for the structured snow shelter. The roots can be made into a serviceable cordage or binding material.
  - ▲ Spruce sap makes an excellent fire starter.

Sycamore *(Platanus occidentalis)*

- ▲ DESCRIPTION: These tall, thickly trunk-ed trees with a wide spreading crown are easy to identify by their camouflage bark. Brittle, flaky bark reveals a more whitish underbark.
- ▲ HABITAT: Sycamores prefer bottom land where they can saturate their roots.
- ▲ RANGE: They are found from Maine to northern Florida.
- ▲ Food: Much like the maple, the sycamore is an excellent source of water.[25]

Tamarack *(Larix laricina)*

- ▲ DESCRIPTION: Tamarack is the only conifer to lose its needles each autumn. These yellow needles make the trees easy to spot at a distance in the fall.
- ▲ HABITAT: Tamaracks can be found in wet, boggy areas as well as open woodlands.
- ▲ RANGE: They range across Canada and the northern United States.

▲ FOOD: Their inner bark, like that of spruces, can be dried, ground, and used as a flour additive.[26]

Watercress *(Nasturtium officinale)*

▲ DESCRIPTION: Watercress can be found throughout the year in dense mats near brooks and springs. Leaflets are small and oval-shaped.

▲ HABITAT: It grows in or near running water.

▲ RANGE: Watercress is found throughout Canada and the United States.

▲ FOOD: This amazing plant offers the winter forager salad greens during the coldest months of the year.[27]

Wild Leek *(Allium tricoccum)*
Wild Onion *(Allium)*

▲ DESCRIPTION: If the winter remains of wild onions (especially leeks) are identified, these plants offer a relative bounty. Look for the dried simple umbel with capsules divided into three parts.

▲ HABITAT: Onions can be found in a variety of habitats including rocky soils, woodland soils, and fields. Leeks prefer the rich, moist soil of deciduous forests.

▲ RANGE: They are found throughout Canada and the United States.

▲ FOOD: The bulbs can be used in the same manner as those of larger, domestic onion varieties.

▲ MEDICINE: Juice from the bulbs can serve as an antiseptic.[28]

Willows *(Salix)*

- ▲ **DESCRIPTION:** Willows range in size from small shrubs to tall, branching trees. It is best to start learning the willow before the winter, when it is in leaf.
- ▲ **HABITAT:** Willows prefer damp roots and are found near streams and moist, wooded areas.
- ▲ **RANGE:** They are found throughout Canada and the United States.
- ▲ **FOOD:** The inner bark can be dried and made into flour.
- ▲ **MEDICINE:** Tea made from willow bark is an effective fever reducer.[29]
- ▲ **UTILITY:**
  - ▲ Willow stems can be used as hand drills, arrows, and basket materials. The inner bark can be used as tinder or twisted into cordage. Willows also make excellent friction fire kits.

▲▲▲▲

105

Winter Cress *(Barbarea vulgaris)*

- ▲ **DESCRIPTION:** Winter cress is one of the earliest late-winter greens. This relative of the mustard plant can be identified by its small, broccoli-like flower clusters.
- ▲ **HABITAT:** It prefers fields and waste ground.
- ▲ **RANGE:** It is found in the northeast and central United States and in southern Canada.
- ▲ **FOOD:** The young leaves and flower heads can be eaten raw or cooked. The flower heads can be added to stews or eaten raw.[30]

▼▼▼

Wintergreen, Checkerberry *(Gaultheria procumbens)*

- ▲ DESCRIPTION: This low-creeping evergreen is often found in evergreen forests.
  Thick leaves are oval and lightly serrated.
- ▲ HABITAT: Checkerberry wintergreen prefers the acidic soils of evergreen forests.
- ▲ RANGE: It extends from Canada through
  the northern United States and south
  along mountain ranges.
- ▲ FOOD: The aromatic leaves can be made
  into tea or chewed fresh.
- ▲ MEDICINE: Wintergreen tea may alleviate
  fever and mild pain.[31]

▲▲▲▲

106

Trapping

The rations of wild edibles found during the winter are often limited and will serve only to slow the rate at which you starve. To subsist over the long term in a winter survival situation (meaning you have little to no gear and food), you must become a proficient trapper. Once set, traps will work for you while you are off tending to other needs. Meat is a caloric-dense food, invaluable to anyone in a time of crisis.

In *Nature's Garden*, Thayer notes that "as one travels north, there tend to be fewer plants with a high MCP (maximum caloric proportion); this is why hunter-gatherers from northern latitudes ate meat for the great majority of their calories."[32] This is especially true during the winter months when the availability of certain resources is limited. Relying solely on plants for sustenance will only forestall starvation. It will not prevent it.

For me, trapping is an ongoing challenge. Even if I don't catch anything, I always learn something new. Maybe my trap was placed in a poor location. Perhaps my trigger wasn't sensitive enough. Trapping is a hands-on activity that can be mastered only from practice.

For years, my skills were limited to knowing how to build a handful of traps with little field experience. Even though I live in a rural area, my concern that I might accidentally catch a neighbor's cat or dog prevented me from proper practice. This led me to start catching animals in a wooden box instead of using a rock for deadfalls (discussed under "Types of Traps"). I also used triggers without a snare or fashioned a snare with weak string. After these changes in my approach, I became much more confident with various trapping mechanisms. In one particular week practicing with a wooden box and various triggers, I caught something every day with a success rate of 100 percent. (I happen to have a cooperative chipmunk that has been caught many times.)

Ethics and Safety

Before we get into the heart of this practice, it is important to state that trapping is to be executed to the best of your ability, meaning you should build a trap that kills your intended target in the most humane manner possible. I find nothing wrong with hunting and trapping as long as it is done within the framework of respect and honor for the animal that will ultimately sacrifice its life for you. It is your responsibility to understand game laws and determine what is and is not allowed in your specific locale. In more places than not, the use of primitive traps is limited to true survival situations where no one would begrudge your trying to provide for yourself in a time of need.

How you practice is important as well. Remain mindful of where you live and the domestic animals that roam through your area. Almost all the elements of learning to trap successfully can be practiced in nonlethal ways if you're willing to be creative. I have a portable deadfall that can be set up in such a way that the weight moves only an inch once an animal has taken the bait (which leaves the animal unharmed). Incorporated into this trap is a wooden base that is designed to hold damp sand or dirt, aiding me in identifying my visitor's tracks.

Traps should be checked daily and dismantled before you leave your area. Exercise extreme caution when setting any kind of trap. Ensure that you stay out of the path of your spring pole in case it releases unexpectedly, and be vigilant when setting up deadfalls so you don't accidentally crush your hand.

A good trap in a poor location will be ineffective. The greater your awareness of animals and their behavior, the more efficient you will become. One benefit of trapping in the winter is that snow makes tracking easier. I love tracking in the snow, following the stories of recent activity.

In New York State, the number of fishers (members of the weasel family) and bobcats is on the rise. (During the writing of this book, in fact, I observed two bobcats near a well-traveled highway in the town of Danby, New York.) Even though I have seen fishers only a handful of times, winter has granted me an intimate understanding of how this animal behaves. In tracking this large mustiled through the snow, I have learned that it loves to walk along logs and zigzag through forests, exploring every tangle and stump along the way.

White-tailed deer, on the other hand, are common in the region where I live. I have been watching and hunting them for years. Without their knowledge, they have even been party to some of my trapping experiments, having set off several types of snare triggers as well as teaching me about bait.

When thinking about trap placement, look for telltale signs such as scat, tracks, hair or fur, dens, or any other indicators of an animal's presence. Transition areas, or places in the landscape where two habitats overlap, are often fruitful places to set up traps. (An example of a transition area would be where a mature forest meets a meadow.) Much like brackish water (where rivers meet the sea), there will come a point where these two habitats collide. Transition areas are attractive to animals because they yield the benefits of two or more ecosystems in such close proximity to one another. Waterways are also excellent places to observe the comings and goings of animals.

Another way of thinking about trap placement is to ask what animals need to survive. Do your best to determine where they procure necessities such as food, shelter, water, and cover. One example of observing animals in this way is the various places where deer choose to bed. Deer prefer a sound vantage point—they like to be able to hear, smell, and see potential threats, so it is critical that they select a location that enables them to take in the big picture.

The Art of Tracking

Tracking is an art, and like any art it takes years to perfect. Volumes have been written on the subject and could easily fill the pages of this book. The advantage of tracking in the winter is that the snow tells a story. A basic knowledge of track identification and animal behavior is critical to becoming a successful trapper.

At its essence, tracking is about observation. As you track, ask yourself the following questions: How many toes do I see? In what direction is the animal traveling? How big is the animal? How and where does it eat? These are but a few of the basic questions you can ask yourself as you unearth clues about what influences an animal's behavior. The weather, time of year, and availability of food and water also impact how and why an animal traverses the landscape.

One way to become familiar with tracks is to view them by family. The following illustrations represent each of the major groups of animals and will aid you in determining, in the most rudimentary fashion, what you're trailing. It is also imperative that you understand each family's pattern when walking. This is especially useful when following animals in deep snow, as tracks have a tendency to fill in. Some animals, like the weasel, are bounders. Hoofed mammals, such as moose, walk in a diagonal pattern. Rabbits gallop, whereas bears walk in a more lumbering fashion.

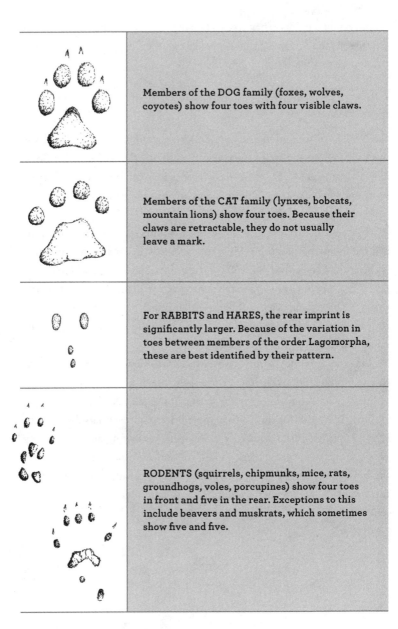

Members of the DOG family (foxes, wolves, coyotes) show four toes with four visible claws.

Members of the CAT family (lynxes, bobcats, mountain lions) show four toes. Because their claws are retractable, they do not usually leave a mark.

For RABBITS and HARES, the rear imprint is significantly larger. Because of the variation in toes between members of the order Lagomorpha, these are best identified by their pattern.

RODENTS (squirrels, chipmunks, mice, rats, groundhogs, voles, porcupines) show four toes in front and five in the rear. Exceptions to this include beavers and muskrats, which sometimes show five and five.

Members of the WEASEL family (martens, otters, weasels, mink, skunks, badgers, fishers) show five toes, often with claw marks.

HOOFED MAMMALS (deer, elk, caribou, moose) are instantly recognizable because of their large, teardrop-shaped symmetrical imprints.

RACCOONS show five toes with claws.

OPOSSUMS, which are the only marsupials in the United States, possess opposable thumbs and leave distinct, human-like prints.

BEARS leave prints that are distinguishable from other tracks in part because of their size. These large mammals hibernate during the winter.

Knots

Before embarking on a discussion of traps and snares, it is essential that you learn and become fluent in knot tying. Although there are hundreds of useful knots, I tend to use only a handful in my outdoor pursuits. The following are versatile and easy to learn and will serve you well with the skills presented in this book. For ease of understanding, most of the illustrations show these knots before they have been tightened. Practice these to the point that they become second nature.

Types of Traps

Trapping is an amalgam of engineering, tracking, knowledge of animal behavior, and experience. Here I will share eight traps that are versatile, easy to construct, and most important, effective. Traps fall into two general categories: deadfalls and snares. They can be either baited or nonbaited. Some traps require rope or cordage and some do not. Baited traps lure an animal into an area with the promise of a reward. Nonbaited traps take advantage of an animal's habits. These are often set along a path or outside of a den where an animal is likely to travel.

When it comes to baiting, it's important to use something that your target animal wants but can't necessarily procure with ease. Finding bait in the winter can be more challenging than in the summer. During the nonwinter months, fruits, minnows, and frogs are in greater abundance. In the winter it is still possible (although much more challenging) to find such things as larvae and fruit.

It is wise to have a knife not only to help you carve traps but also to fashion various lengths of cordage. Your survival kit may include rope (or even cable) to assist with larger animal snares. Bait should also be included in your kit. A classic staple is peanut butter. This should be purchased in foil packets and sealed within plastic bags to ensure that animals don't turn your bait into a free meal—or run away with your pack!

When it comes to baiting a trap, it's important to make your animal work for it. If an apple is shoved onto a bait stick, it's possible that an animal will gnaw at it but never set off the trap. I like to split my bait sticks at the end, shove the bait into the cracks, and cover it with a bit of cordage. This ensures that the animal will pull and push on the bait stick, ultimately setting off the trap.

A "bait pit" is a sound practice tool: you leave bait in a sandy area and go back to investigate what tracks have been left behind and what foods have been appropriated. I once worked at a nature center in the Berkshire Mountains of Massachusetts. The staff, along with our students, left bits of food in a sandbox near our compost bins. Each morning we would check to see who had visited. This was fairly predictable, with appearances by chipmunks, squirrels, and the occasional porcupine. One morning, however, we awoke to see the tracks of a black bear. We later saw this bear and a companion sitting in our compost bins.

DEADFALLS

Deadfalls are traps that crush an animal with either a rock or a log. The deadfall is held up with a trigger (sometimes baited, sometimes not), which is released by the targeted species. It's important that your deadfall be wide and heavy enough to quickly dispatch any animal. As a general rule, use the heaviest weight that your targeted animal can release. A thirty-pound rock may seem like overkill for a red squirrel, but this helps ensure the effectiveness of the trap if it is tripped by a larger animal such as a snowshoe hare. Ideally you want your triggers sensitive enough to be set off by a small animal but heavy enough to take care of a larger visitor.

It is also important to stabilize your deadfall to ensure that when it falls, it lands on either solid ground or a flat rock. If using a rock, make sure it rests squarely on the ground and doesn't shift under pressure. Once set, your deadfall rock should be at approximately a thirty-degree angle. The baited end of your trigger stick should be centered under your deadfall and positioned underneath, toward the back third of the mechanism. Once mastered, these traps can be used in a variety of situations.

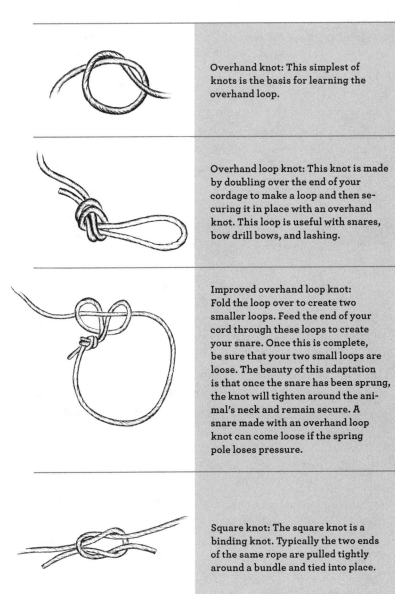

Overhand knot: This simplest of knots is the basis for learning the overhand loop.

Overhand loop knot: This knot is made by doubling over the end of your cordage to make a loop and then securing it in place with an overhand knot. This loop is useful with snares, bow drill bows, and lashing.

Improved overhand loop knot: Fold the loop over to create two smaller loops. Feed the end of your cord through these loops to create your snare. Once this is complete, be sure that your two small loops are loose. The beauty of this adaptation is that once the snare has been sprung, the knot will tighten around the animal's neck and remain secure. A snare made with an overhand loop knot can come loose if the spring pole loses pressure.

Square knot: The square knot is a binding knot. Typically the two ends of the same rope are pulled tightly around a bundle and tied into place.

Clove hitch: The clove hitch is typically used to fasten cord or rope to rails or poles.

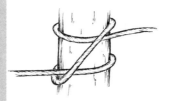

Timber hitch: The timber hitch is a simple yet effective hitch with many applications. It can be used to bundle materials together as you transport them to your shelter. It is also a good knot for use with lashing projects.

Half hitch: The simplest of hitches, the half hitch is commonly used to finish lashing projects and secure excess cord on bow drill bows. Two half hitches are commonly used together to add security to projects.

Improved clench knot: This knot is used to secure a fish hook or lure to monofilament. It can be used in other ways, such as when a cord needs to be secured and remain fixed to an object.

The Figure Four

The figure four is a classic deadfall that does not require cordage and is extremely stable. Although I have chosen to include this popular trap, in its standard form I have experienced several deficiencies that have yet to be thoroughly examined. Still, it embodies many important lessons and fundamental challenges that you might encounter as a trapper.

This trap's trigger system comprises the three interlocking components shown in the illustration. The required notches must be cut with great care. Because the bait stick is attached on one side of the upright, this trap must be triggered from the proper location, meaning that the animal needs to pull the bait stick off the upright. If your target approaches from the wrong side, the typical result is that the triggering mechanism turns and the bait ends up outside (and not underneath) your deadfall.

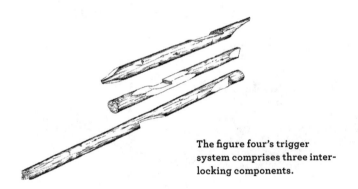

The figure four's trigger system comprises three interlocking components.

Another problem with the figure four is that an animal may push down on the bait stick while taking the bait, failing to spring the trap.

I often incorporate several modifications to the classic figure four to alleviate these problems. First, a fence or barrier can be included to ensure that your target approaches the trap from the correct side. Second, the bottom of the upright can be extended, squared off, and stuck in the ground. Securing the upright in this way makes it stable and therefore less likely to turn when an animal pulls on the bait stick. Third, I will

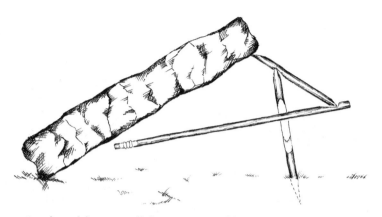

Simple modifications will eliminate any problems the figure four poses.

sometimes modify the upright so that this trap can be sprung if the animal pushes down on the bait stick as well as if it pulls the bait stick to the side.

The Paiute

I love this trap because of its simplicity and effectiveness. I have used this system successfully many times and in various ways. It can be used as a trigger for snares as well. The Paiute looks much like the figure four. I prefer the John McPherson style of Paiute, which is made without the aid of a knife. When using the Paiute, it is important to keep the following in mind: this is a highly sensitive trap that will spring if the bait stick is moved in any direction. When setting the bait stick, one end pushes against the small toggle while the other end finds a rough spot or a small indentation on the underside of the deadfall. The bait stick that is used for the Paiute is generally made from a weedy plant such as goldenrod or wild mustard, so splitting your stick for bait application may prove difficult. As an alternative, I simply wrap my bait in cordage.

A Paiute-style trigger can be used in many different ways. The second illustration shows this simple yet effective mechanism without a snare. With some creativity, this trigger can be used vertically along trails and at den sites.

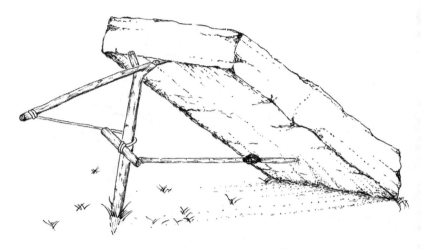

The Paiute is a model of simplicity and effectiveness.

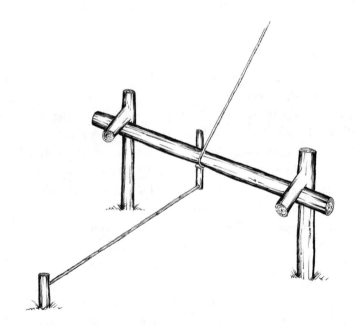

A Paiute-style trigger can be modified to suit your needs.

The Two-Stick Deadfall

One of my favorite traps is the two-stick deadfall. This simple trap can be made without the use of a knife and requires no cordage. The upright, which is usually beveled at the top, sits on the ground. The bait stick is beveled at the top where it sits on top of the upright. When the animal pulls down on the baited end, the upright is forced away and the deadfall is released.

Although this trap is simplicity personified, there are several variables to be aware of. First, you must test this trap by pushing down on the bait stick. I have found that it is possible to have the trigger stick pushed all the way to the ground without forcing the upright to move. Look for the "sweet spot" where everything comes together. Experiment with the angle of the upright, the length of the bait stick, and the spot where the bait stick rests on the upright. Once it is set properly, this trap is quite effective.

▲▲▲▲

119

Cordage is not used in the construction of the two-stick deadfall.

The Athabaskan Log Deadfall

This trap lures the target animal into a baited corral or can be used at den sites. When the animal enters the corral, it steps down on the trigger stick, releasing a heavy deadfall log. This trap can be designed for a variety of game. You secure the "keeper" stick to the log by twisting it tight with a loop of cordage. It is then held in place with the trigger stick.

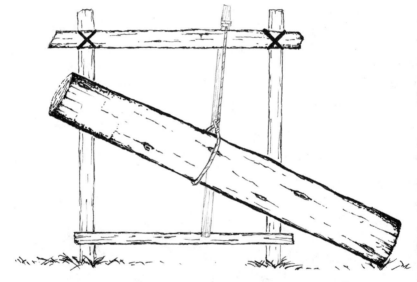

The Athabaskan log deadfall often utilizes a baited corral.

SNARES

Snares generally utilize a bent sapling or a pole that will lift or spring an animal off the ground via a noose. Some snares, however, are designed to simply detain. Simple wire loops can be set along rabbit runs. Set each snare with a specific animal in mind. Test your snare pole beforehand to ensure that it is powerful enough to perform to your needs. Dead poles and saplings maintain their springiness better than living trees.

When setting snares along runs, look for natural funnels where the topography or foliage gives the animal little choice but to stay on the trail. Size your snare so that the opening is large enough for the head of your intended quarry. Once the head slips through the noose, the trap is sprung as the animal detaches the spring pole (rolling snare) or releases a trigger that trips the pole (T-bar snare).

The Rolling Snare
The rolling snare is a simple spring pole snare that is set along a trail or run. The illustration shows how this basic snare is constructed. Wire is convenient for use with small game, as it maintains its shape. When using cordage, you may have to keep your loop in place by using small Y sticks.

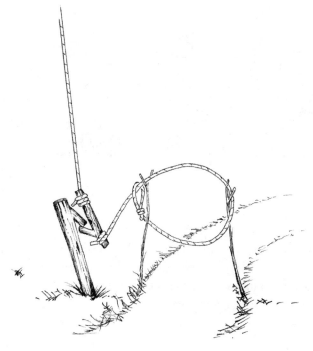

The rolling snare is most effective when set along a trail or run.

The T-Bar Snare

This is a snare of lethal design whereby an animal is drawn to the baited end of the T-shaped trigger stick. This trigger stick is placed inside a corral of sticks, and the noose is placed on top. When the animal lifts up on the bait stick, it triggers the snare. With some creativity, this can also be used without bait at den sites. Again, be careful about the size of your opening.

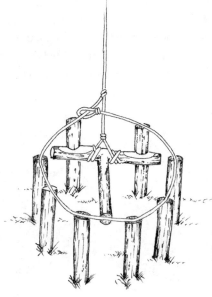

The size of your opening is crucial to success with the T-bar snare.

The first time I tested this trap was in suburban Buffalo, New York, when I was trying to catch a gray squirrel. I baited my T-bar with peanut butter and was able to observe from a window as the animal approached. It looked as though all was going according to plan. The squirrel put its head into the corral, but the opening was so voluminous that he stepped into the enclosed area with one leg. When the trap sprang, the squirrel found itself dangling in the air with the noose around its shoulder. It quickly gnawed its way free.

The Deer Snare

This snare will restrain but not necessarily kill, so you must be prepared to dispatch any trapped animals. The figure shows how this can be used along a deer trail. The beauty of this snare is that it can be tripped from either direction. I have learned that as long as you have strong enough rope or cable, snaring deer can be easier than catching small game. A rabbit,

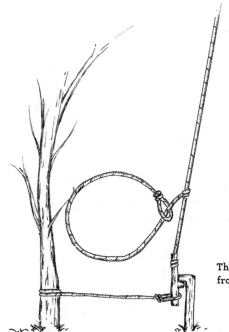

▲▲▲▲

123

The deer snare can be tripped from either direction.

unlike a hoofed mammal, doesn't have a long neck. A deer, by contrast, will have its entire head through this snare before the trigger is tripped.

THE ARAPUCA

The Arapuca uses a basket instead of a deadfall to live catch birds. The first time I experimented with this triggering system, my sons and I caught two redpolls. These are petite birds, a testament to the trap's sensitivity. The basket portion of this trap is a unique design. It can be made using two pieces of cord and an ample supply of straight sticks. Bait can be attached to both bait sticks or simply piled underneath the basket. All that is required for the basket to fall is for one of the bait sticks to be tripped.

Ice Fishing

Catching fish is another viable option when you're looking to fill the stew pot during winter. As a youth I remember catching pan fish and bass through the ice on Boy Scout campouts. We used an auger to drill holes through the ice and used grubs as bait and modern fishhooks and line on our poles. For this reason, I would recommend including basic fishing gear in your survival kit. Be sure to pack small jigs made specifically for ice fishing, as well as an assortment of hooks and weights (and line, of course). Rods, if desired, can easily be fashioned from the branches of trees.

Years ago, one of my youth groups and I experimented with a hot rock to determine if we could melt a hole through the ice of a pond where we ran a weekly Primitive Pursuits program. Participants gathered wood and built a substantial fire. We placed a large, melon-sized piece of granite in the fire and additional wood was added. We let the fire heat up until the rock was glowing red. We then carried our rock to a promising spot and set it down on the ice. The ice steamed and melted, and soon the rock was sitting in a large pit of water. Within minutes our rock dropped through the ice and we had a suitable hole through which to fish.

Preparing Your Catch

Regardless of your catch—mammal, fish, or fowl—butchering is about getting to the meat and putting all inedible parts aside for other potential uses. When doing so, be sure not to cut open any part of the digestive tract. You should also be careful to avoid contact with the animal's blood

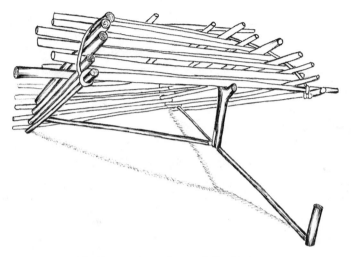

The Arapuca is used to catch live birds.

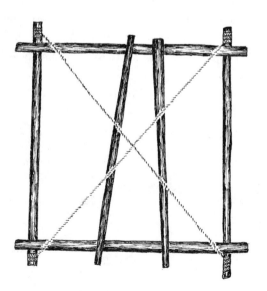

The basket portion of the Arapuca comprises nothing more
than cordage and straight sticks.

if you have any open cuts or sores.

Begin by hanging your catch with the head down, making an incision beneath the anus and sexual organs. Cut through until you have penetrated the lower tract. Remember to slice through the hide but not into the internal organs, and work your way down toward the rib cage. Please note that cutting through the rib cage of a larger animal can be difficult. If this is too hard, simply cut up and through the hide. Now carefully make an incision around the anus.

At the other end, near the head, cut through the trachea and esophagus. If you have been unsuccessful in penetrating the rib cage, you may need to reach through the animal's body to access this area. With some elbow grease, you will now be able to remove the entrails. The one advantage to preparing your catch in the winter is that, assuming temperatures are below forty degrees, spoiling is not a pressing issue. You will, however, need to keep your game stowed away from other animals.

Birds should be plucked, as they are more flavorful and of greater nutritional value with their skins left intact. Fish can be scaled, although I often cook mine with the skin on and worry about removing it later.

Mammals must have their hides removed. This is a simple process. Start by cutting through the skin above each foot and below the head. With little effort, the hides of most animals can be removed by pulling at them with your hands. If you need to use a knife, be careful not to cut

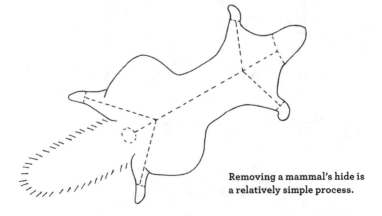

**Removing a mammal's hide is
a relatively simple process.**

or slice the hide.

Remember that an animal should be utilized to its fullest extent. Beyond a good meal (remember to cook your game thoroughly), an animal offers the survivalist many resources. Hides can be tanned into leather or used as rawhide. Feathers can be used for fletching or insulation. Bones can be made into an assortment of tools, including knives, awls, and arrowheads. Sinew, which is an incredibly strong fiber, can be dried, pounded, and fashioned into cordage. Any inedible entrails can be used as bait to entice your next meal.

Exercises

1. Make a habit of finding comfortable places in the woods and other wild spaces to sit quietly for as long as you can. Remember that the way you enter a wild place will impact the environment—how you amble through the woods will either repel animals or enable you to pass by unnoticed. Make note of how the wildlife around you move about the forest. Do they tell you anything about where to forage or shelter? What about their habits might aid you in constructing traps or snares? Do the tracks they leave tell a story?

2. Choose the following plants from the above list to identify: cattail, mustard, and watercress. Harvest these plants and include them as part of your evening meal. Note their abundance and the ease or difficulty with which they are procured. Are the cattail's tubers a suitable reward when weighed against the risk of possible wet feet? Are mustards more plentiful than other species? Do you prefer the greenery that, even in the harshest of winters, watercress provides?

3. Embark on an ice-fishing excursion from start to finish, being sure to abide by all regional conservation laws. Make a fire, heat rocks, melt a hole through the ice, and then clean and pan-sear your catch. Although fish are a good source of protein, does your yield justify the time and

effort you've expended? Is fishing a luxury when compared with trapping or foraging, or is this more a question of locale?

Chapter 6

Helpful Crafts and Skills

The crust soon melted and they sank up to their thighs
in the soft powder.... Fito Strauch, their inventor, discovered ...
that if cushions from the passenger seats were tied to their
boots, they made passable snowshoes.

Piers Paul Read, *Alive*

On assignment for *Life in the Finger Lakes* magazine in August of 2012, Jon shadowed Primitive Pursuits' Forest Archer program. Of all the skills he observed, he was most taken with a demonstration of knapping—the practice and art of shaping rock.

Jon watched as lead instructor Justin Sutera flaked apart pieces of obsidian to create stone carving tools. Later, Sutera used these tools to skin a groundhog. Utilizing resources the earth provided, he was able to remove the animal's pelt in less than twenty minutes.[1]

The deeper an outdoorsman's bag of tricks—coupled with true hands-on experience—the more options he will have at his disposal. Our forebears met seasonal challenges not with apprehension but with confidence. The skills culled from our collective ancestry are indeed vast, and learning these will deepen your connection with nature like nothing else can.

Coal Burning

Coal burning is an incredibly important skill to master. This skill, which has been used to fashion items as large as canoes, allows you to make wooden bowls that can then be used to boil water. The importance of being able to purify water with this method should not be underestimated. I have coal-burned numerous containers and spoons over the years. With care, these projects will last for years.

The easiest way to begin a coal-burning project is to use a saw and ax. Look for sections of wood that are free of knots or other imperfections. My favorite woods for coal burning are cedar, basswood, aspen, and pine, but any soft wood will do. These materials should be dead, dry, and free of knots or cracks. In a true survival situation, you will not likely have metal tools at your disposal. In such cases, simply burn a section of wood to length and use this uncut, rounded portion for your project. (Logs are typically split in half for coal burning, but without the luxury of metal tools, burning the round is a viable alternative.)

The hardest part of any coal-burning project is getting started. To begin, place your coals in the center where you want your catch to be. These coals, with a well-directed exhale, will heat up and your project will soon begin to smolder. In no time your log will turn red with heat. Remember that you are the artist. Much like a sculptor wielding her chisel, you will determine where wood burns away by the placement of coals. Quite often the interior of your bowl will become red hot and embers will no longer be required. Burning can then be controlled by dampening certain areas. Wind can be a great ally when it comes to coal burning.

One thing to avoid is flames. While coals are relatively easy to control, flames will lick the edge of your container, rendering it nothing more than a charred piece of wood. Be careful not to go too far and burn your bowl through the bottom. Once you're satisfied with it, scrape it clean using a stick or smooth rock.

Be sure to start your fire and your coal-burning projects as soon as you've established your camp. Once your fire is burning, you can get your project going and monitor its progress while tending to other matters. I once left a large split willow log out overnight with a small pile of coals in the center. In the morning, I was fortunate enough to find that my project hadn't burned through but had converted into a functional bowl.

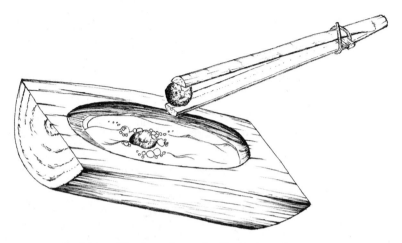

Coal-burned bowls can be used to heat and purify water.

Pine Bark Baskets

The Eastern white pine is a gift to the survivalist. This magnificent tree can be found throughout the Northeast, the Great Lakes, and south along the Appalachian Mountains. The bark of this conifer can be removed and folded into a seamless container that can then be used for cooking or water purification. These containers can also be used directly over a bed of coals. When I use them in this way, I prefer to buffer the container by placing green sticks on the coals and my container on top. This will, however, diminish the life of your container. Unlike most barks that lend themselves to basket making, white pine bark can be removed from the tree in the winter and, once removed, is leathery and pliable, making it ideal to fold and manipulate.

The best bark to use for this project comes from either young trees or lower branches. The bark should be smooth and without damage. The older, more mature bark of the white pine is rough. I typically locate a section of bark from a branch that is at least fourteen inches in diameter and of substantial length. Using a knife, make two circular cuts around each end of your length of bark. Next, make a straight cut lengthwise connecting these circular cuts. When hammering through the bark, make sure that you've cut down all the way through the bark and into the wood.

This next step is helpful but not always necessary. Heat your wood next to the fire. (Heating the bark will make it easier to remove.) Be sure to turn your project regularly to ensure that all sides are evenly heated. (Removing pine bark in the winter without the aid of heat can be done, but it is challenging.) Next, using a spatula (a small, flattened hardwood stick), gently pry up a corner of your bark. Be careful not to poke through the bark! Instead, carefully use this tool to separate the bark from the wood. If all goes well, you'll end up with a rectangular sheet.

You can fashion simple pins to secure the corners of your pine bark basket by splitting a short stick. I like to bind one end of a three-inch stick (about one inch in circumference) or find a stick that branches or has a knot at one end. This branching or knotted end will help prevent your split from going all the way through and doesn't require any binding.

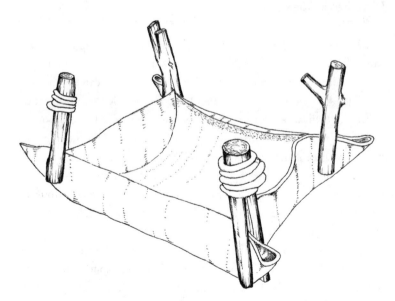

To construct a white pine bark container, secure
each corner in place with a split stick.

Tongs

I often craft tongs because they are so useful in handling hot rocks and coals. I tend to use green wood, looking for material that's straight, several inches in diameter, and at least eighteen inches in length. Certain woods split straighter than others. I prefer to use ash and cedar for my tongs. Once your wood is split, shove a small stone in the crack toward the base and secure this in place with a length of cord. The cord also prevents the tongs from splitting.

Snow Saws

Snow saws or knives were traditionally made of bone and wood for use in the construction of igloos. In lieu of carrying a modern snow saw, you can improvise a useful cutting tool from wood. I often use a simple snow saw that my older son made for me years ago. This tool can be crafted from split wood or a large, flat splinter from a damaged tree. Remember, too, that you can quarry and remove snow blocks from drifts using something as rudimentary as a straight stick.

▲▲▲▲

133

Wooden saws can be used to quarry blocks of snow.

Stone Tools and Knapping

Rocks, our geological record, can be used in a variety of ways to help complete certain tasks. From pounders to hammers, scrapers to sanders, they are an invaluable resource. Always remain vigilant and keep an eye out for these hidden gems. With snow cover, this can be challenging.

To combat this, I typically look to stream and creek beds, steep areas, or overhangs where snow is less likely to accumulate. Here I will focus on creating basic edged tools.

Becoming an expert at making sharp-edged stone tools can take years. With that said, it is important to understand that simple and effective tools can be made quickly in times of need. With a basic understanding of how to work stone, these wedges, simple knives, and choppers and scrapers can be made with minimal effort. This process is called knapping.

The best rocks to use for sharper-edged tools are those with a high silica content. Obsidian is a classic example of this type of stone. The easiest way to find suitable rocks is to look for dense stone that has a high-pitched ring when you tap it with a rounded, hammer-like stone. The higher the ring, the better suited the rock is for making sharp-edged tools. As always, experiment. I have made tools from slate, even though sedimentary rock isn't thought of as ideal knapping material.

Exercise caution when working with stone. If you don't have eye protection (such as ski goggles), close your eyes before striking your rock. Once you've found a stone, support it either on your lap or in your non-dominant hand. Using a hammer stone (a hard, rounded cobble), forcefully strike the edge with a glancing blow, directing your effort on a spot near the bottom half of your rock. Be sure to continue your motion and follow through. If all has gone well, you will release a flake from your stone. Depending on its size, this flake can be used as a splitting wedge, a chopper, or a knife. Experiment with this method of removing flakes. Adjust the angle of your strike, the angle at which you hold your larger tool rock, and the force with which you strike.

Stone tools have a multitude of uses.

Digging Sticks

The digging stick is a simple tool used to loosen soil and extract tubers and roots from the earth. It is a hardwood stick two to two and a half feet in length that is beveled at one end. Under certain conditions it may become necessary to thaw prospective areas with a fire before digging.

The digging stick is a simple yet effective tool.

Footwear

Proper footwear is essential to the itinerant survivalist. Here I share three of my favorite designs.

Improvised Snow Shoes

The use of snow shoes may become necessary to facilitate travel through deep snow. Snow shoes can be as simple as lashing spruce branches underneath your feet. These are then bound near the toe. With the luxury of cordage, fancier snowshoes can be crafted out of saplings. The illustration shows the classic Tom Roycroft design for making snowshoes in the backcountry.

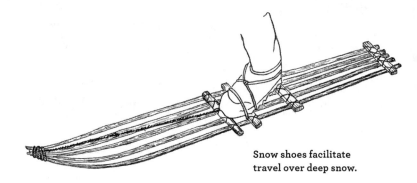

Snow shoes facilitate
travel over deep snow.

Expandable Moccasins

In an issue of the now-defunct magazine *Wilderness Way*, Randal Jones
contributed an excellent article titled "The Perfect 15-Minute Moccasin," wherein he described a design from the Tierra Del Fuegan Indians.
These people, who lived in the archipelago region south of mainland
South America, adapted footwear to an unpredictable environment with
an average summer temperature of only fifty degrees.[2]

These moccasins are easy to make, and they expand and contract to
receive natural insulation such as grasses and sedges. The illustration
shows how to use your foot to create a moccasin specific to your needs.
(The overall pattern should be the length of two of your feet, with the
lower width the length of your foot and the upper portion the width of
your foot from the big toe to the little toe. Depending on the temperature,
you may want to expand on this design to accommodate more insulation.)

First, fold the pattern's heel section in half and sew these two pieces
together. After placing your foot in the pattern, punch holes where your
foot meets the ankle. Then fold the remaining part of the pattern over the
top of your foot to where the foot meets the ankle. Last, punch matching
holes in the upper portion as depicted in the illustration and lace your
moccasins in a drawstring fashion.

Although these moccasins are ideally made from leather, they can be

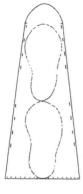

Moccasins are often insulated with grasses or sedges. This pattern uses your foot to determine the moccasin's proportions.

made from other materials such as car seat covers or canvas and adapted to beef up lighter footwear. I have constructed several pairs of these over the years and believe they are truly the perfect moccasin. I often add uppers to my design, transforming them into a mukluk-style shoe.

▲▲▲▲

137

The moccasin on the left includes the addition of uppers, has been fully insulated, and is laced in a crisscross fashion. The moccasin on the right is noninsulated and has been drawn tight to be snug on the foot.

Netting

When Ötzi the Ice Man, whose remains date back to the late Neolithic period, was discovered in the Ötztal Alps in September of 1991, he was wearing leather shoes insulated with grasses. This grass layer was held in place with a net. (Because his footwear was insulated with hay, Ötzi was thought to have been a migratory herder.) Such an intricately designed piece of footwear reflected the ingenuity and needs of a people who lived in a harsh and unforgiving environment.[3]

With Ötzi as my inspiration, I once crafted a handmade net and filled this with grasses to bolster the poor footwear of one of my students. As a means of comparison, we insulated one foot and left the other in her sneaker. The results were alarming—the bundled foot was warm and comfortable, whereas the noninsulated foot was significantly colder.

Netting is an age-old skill found across the globe. Once understood, making netting is a relaxing process that results in a craft that has many uses. The figure shows one way to make netting using overhand knots.

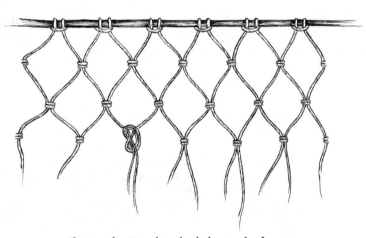

The use of netting dates back thousands of years.

Exercises

1. Fashion a coal-burned bowl and pine bark container, and then experiment boiling water in each. Which is easier to construct? Which is more durable? Which is better suited for travel?

2. Assemble footwear during a simulated situation involving a stranded vehicle. First, remove the cover from a seat cushion without the aid of a knife. Secure this in place with cordage or netting and fill with grasses or other insulation. Then walk a mile over snowy, uneven terrain and record the results.

3. Visit a nearby creek or stream and survey the area for rocks that are suitable for boiling and knapping. Are such rocks abundant in number? If you are not able to locate rocks with a high silica content, experiment with knapping sedimentary rocks such as shale. Put the resulting flakes to use trimming meat, skinning game, or slicing edibles.

Chapter 7

Navigation and Orienteering

The hard snow held me, save where now and then
One foot went down. The view was all in lines
Straight up and down of tall slim trees
Too much alike to mark or name a place by
So as to say for certain I was here
Or somewhere else: I was just far from home.

Robert Frost, "The Wood-Pile"

Shortly after graduating from college, a friend and I took an extended backpacking trip through Glacier National Park in Montana. Even though we were entering summer, portions of the park were covered in deep snow. As a precaution, we took along topographic maps to aid us in our journey.

Understanding how important it was that we not venture off course, my friend and I studied our maps to avoid any unseen pitfalls. This was one of the more epochal moments in my lifetime as a naturalist, and I attribute much of my future success to the sensible planning and sound navigational skills I honed on this expedition.

What to Do before Embarking on Any Outdoor Adventure

The more remote the wilderness area you encounter, the greater the risk of becoming lost if you venture from established footpaths. Without question, a short walk down a county lane is far different from a weekend trek into the White Mountains. For those who have never been lost in the wilderness, it can be a terrifying experience. The trees, which moments before were regarded as welcome companions, become beings of insidious intent, closing in on you at every turn.

To avoid falling into the grip of panic, be deliberate about your itinerary, the survival gear you choose to bring, and your planned course and estimated time of arrival. Leave a detailed agenda with at least one person who will miss you if you don't return as intended. On my own excursions, this includes my wife and if I'm embarking on a work-related trip, my supervisor. When hiking established trails, be sure to sign the register at the trailhead, including your full name, the date, and time. In most situations, government agencies will have your itinerary if a permit is required. You should provide all relevant information to someone even if you are on a road trip.

The information you leave with loved ones should include

- Where you are going
- The trailhead's name and location
- A map with trails and campsite locations as well as the dates you expect to reach each site
- A brief description of your daily agenda. (If you are staying at a base camp each night but intend to go out hiking each day, include this as well.)
- Your cell phone number and the numbers of local rangers and law enforcement agencies
- The make, model, license plate number, and color of your vehicle
- The name, age, and contact information of everyone in your group

If you are stranded, disoriented, or lost, it is my hope that you will have done your homework and become proficient in the skills detailed in this book. If you believe yourself to be lost, it is best to stop, take a deep breath, and retrace your steps. (If there is snow on the ground, retracing your steps will be a decidedly more surmountable task, assuming your tracks haven't been erased by wind or subsequent snowfall.) When retracing your steps is impractical—snow is absent or you're caught in whiteout conditions—begin by assessing your needs. As time and resources permit, you will procure the items necessary for survival.

Most individuals who are reported lost in the wilderness are found within seventy-two hours. There are survival schools that bank on this statistic, teaching people how to address their most immediate needs with the understanding that help is on the way. To me, this attitude seems short-sighted. Not only does it propagate a fear of nature, but it helps only marginally. If faced with a long-term situation where rescue is unlikely, you will be well served by having taken the time to learn the skills presented in this book.

Walking Out versus Staying Put

If you find yourself lost or stranded and are likely to be reported missing, search-and-rescue (SAR) teams will want you to do the following:

- ▲ STAY PUT! (And stay together if you are in a group.) Don't wander, but by all means move to take advantage of natural resources as well as open areas that increase your visibility.
- ▲ HELP YOURSELF. Make fire, construct shelter, secure water, assess your resources (manmade as well as natural), and put these to use.
- ▲ MAKE IT EASY TO BE SEEN AND HEARD. Be ready with a signal fire, and remember that three is the universal sign for help (three orange flags, three whistle blasts, etc.).

After a storm came through our area a few years ago, I had all my students collect fallen hemlock branches. Once we had amassed a large pile, we dropped it on our already raging fire. The smoke was plentiful and thick, lasting a good five minutes. In a true survival situation, a signal fire could mean the difference between life and death.

Walking out of a true wilderness survival situation is a monumental decision—particularly during the winter. Leaving the relative comfort of your camp and traversing the unknown poses inherent risks, but under certain circumstances it may be exactly what you have to do.

There are generally three sound reasons to walk out:

- No one has probable cause to know where you are.
- You are off course.
- It's been too long.

NO ONE HAS PROBABLE CAUSE TO KNOW WHERE YOU ARE. If you have neglected to provide your itinerary to a trusted friend or family member and you find yourself lost during an outing, there is no reason to believe that someone will know where to look for you. If you've done nothing other than sign in at the trail register with a brief description of your plans, this may help you eventually. Registers are not checked daily, and rangers do not scour the woods for people who have not signed out. Plenty of people forget to sign out of the woods! If you are reported missing, your name, a description of your vehicle, and other important details will find their way into the hands of authorities. By the time this happens, however, a week may have passed. Don't be foolish. Under circumstances where no one is likely to know where you are, hiking out may be your best (and only) option.

YOU ARE OFF COURSE. If you've determined that you are off course, hiking out may become a necessity. How far is too far? Imagine walking five miles off course. Initial search-and-rescue efforts will focus on the most probable areas for success. As efforts continue, the search radius expands but becomes less detailed for the simple reason that there is a greater area within the search grid. SAR personnel will eventually come to the conclusion that you are outside the initial search area but may have few clues as to which direction you've traveled. Five miles, which is a modest distance on foot, opens up a huge search area. It's difficult to deduce how far off course is too far, but at some point you may have to come to terms with the fact that you will have to save yourself.

IT'S BEEN TOO LONG. After three days under adverse winter conditions, operations quickly turn into body recovery efforts. Keeping SAR personnel safe is important to all involved. Once it has been determined that the likelihood of survival is minimal, the welfare of rescuers becomes a priority. If four or more days have passed and no one has found you, you will want to consider walking out.

When deciding to walk out, avoid impulsivity. Although you might be anxious to return to civilization, the quick decision is not always the judicious one. Weigh your options and use the resources at your disposal to determine the most reasonable course of action. Think of each day as the beginning of a new survival situation—you will likely have to create fire and shelter anew before the end of each day that you travel, so be sure to allow time for this.

In *Alive*, the story of the Uruguayan rugby team whose plane crashed in the Andes, the survivors had every reason to believe that they were on their own. Although aircraft were spotted above the crash site, the white fuselage was difficult (if not impossible) to see from the air. Survivors ultimately spent seventy-two days on the mountain before they were rescued. (To facilitate and ensure their survival, two expeditionaries from the team hiked to the base of the mountain over a grueling nine-day period.)

Before heading out, ask yourself the following:

- ▲ Am I adequately prepared?
- ▲ If I leave my current situation, will I be better off?
- ▲ Will I survive if I leave?
- ▲ Will I survive if I stay?

Take time to prepare and use all your resources to the best of your ability. Walking out could be the most important decision of your life. If you haven't already, this is the time to wrap up any loose ends. Be sure that, if you don't have a modern fire-lighting device, you carry smoldering punky wood and be ready to make a signal fire at a moment's notice. Leave a trail as you go to indicate your direction. You can build cairns, flag, or leave other signs as to your whereabouts. (While lost in the Maine wilderness, Bill Bryson's hiking companion, Stephen Katz, left an empty pack of Old Gold cigarettes to signal that he had found his way back to the trail.)

So you've decided to walk out. Which way do you go? Remember, the larger the wilderness area you've entered, the greater the potential for error. The following suggestions won't necessarily work if you're in a "never-ending" wilderness area such as Alaska. Many of these techniques will work by virtue of the fact that our planet is highly populated and you will eventually encounter someone in your sojourns.

Going Straight Is Good!

There is an old riddle that asks, "How far can you run into the woods?" The answer is halfway. Once you're halfway through, you're then running out of the woods. This riddle can help you if you can keep from walking in circles.

Over terrain where the landscape doesn't dictate their course of travel, people are prone to walking in circles. In my own programs I have blindfolded students at the edge of an open field and asked them to walk in a straight line. Some students have circled back on their trail in an area smaller than a basketball court. It is the rare student who can walk without curving one way or the other. If you can stay on a straight course, you will eventually get out of the woods, hit a road, or emerge near some form of civilization.

The following techniques and devices will keep you from walking in circles:

- ▲ Straight-line sighting
- ▲ Three-object straight-line sighting
- ▲ Following waterways

- Sun sticks
- Maps, compasses, and GPS units

Straight-Line Sighting

Straight-line sighting is simply finding an object in the distance and walking toward it. This object should be as far away as possible and easy to distinguish. Keep in mind that this technique can be difficult to implement in thickly wooded areas. Jon used straight-line sighting to find his way out of the forest during what he had assumed would be a routine hike:

One afternoon my wife and I took our greyhound on a hike through the Finger Lakes National Forest in Hector, New York. This particular stretch of trail winds through the woods and into a pasture before returning to the woods and ending near a patch of blueberry bushes. Portions of this hike are breathtaking; depending on the time of year, you can stand under an apple tree and forage as you gaze into the valley below. We had completed the bulk of our hike and, in a moment of laxity, became lost in conversation.

My wife and I entered an area where the path wasn't clearly defined, as areas of the forest floor were devoid of cover. Before we realized what had happened, we were lost. There was no sign of the familiar blue blazes that to this point had marked our journey. In all likelihood, we had changed course.

With dusk closing in, we decided that instead of trying to find the trail we would hike due west where I knew a seasonal dirt road cut through the expanse. (Although we were without a compass, we simply looked in the direction of the sun.) I made note of a towering pine in the distance and we began walking.

It was a more arduous hike than either of us had anticipated. We entered a dense swath of undergrowth and had to carry our dog to avoid entangling his leash. As the sun dipped toward

Using a trio of objects to create a straight line is an effective means of finding your way out of the woods.

the horizon, we discussed the possibility of bedding down for the night and resuming our efforts in the morning.

Just as we had resigned ourselves to this fate, I spotted what appeared to be a clearing up ahead. We emerged onto the road as the sun slipped out of sight, tired and hungry but little worse for wear.

Three-Object Straight-Line Sighting

This technique requires you to identify three objects in a row and use them to travel in a straight path. For example, find a prominent boulder that's in line with a stump, and find a third object in the distance such as a small evergreen. Make sure that the objects you choose are in a straight line. Walk toward the middle object. When you get to the middle object, look back at your first object and forward to your third to ensure that you are still on course. From this middle object, look past your evergreen and find a new third object that's in line with your other landmarks. In this way you will be able to leapfrog your way out of the wilderness. If you're in a group, members of your party can act as markers and be directed to move ahead, stop, and bear left or right to ensure proper alignment.

Following Waterways

Every waterway, no matter how small, leads to the ocean. At my house we have a small, spring-fed stream that flows past my barn. On its downhill journey, this joins another stream on the adjacent property and gains strength. When it reaches the valley at the bottom of the hill, this joins a larger creek that is rich with signs of life—beaver, muskrat, and a diverse assortment of birds make their home in this habitat.

This wetland then drains into more substantial waterways, eventually joining the Susquehanna River, which empties into the Chesapeake Bay. Along its journey, the water that started in the woods behind my home crosses paths with civilization, going under roads, paralleling highways, and flowing past all manner of settlements. As long as you know your general location—meaning you're not stranded in British Columbia, where the drainage basin flows through completely wild places on its journey to the sea—following waterways is a good idea.

This technique comes with a few cautions. Waterways can be dangerous. At no time should you compromise your safety when using this technique. Stay away from steep banks, unsafe ice, or wetlands where you could get bogged down. Creeks and rivers can also lead to large lakes where it can be difficult to find an outlet. It's possible, however, to keep an eye on the landscape and be aware of where the drainage flows without being directly in a valley. Use common sense.

If you are not in sight of a waterway, move downhill. You are more than likely to run into something. Jon has also used this method to find his way out of the woods:

As part of a youth program I was coordinating, years ago I

invited Primitive Pursuits to facilitate a course in wilderness survival near my home in Newfield, New York. We established our base camp in a natural area near Chaffee Creek, a modest waterway that weaves through a vast stretch of State Forest. This area is remote, but our shelter, which was only a ten-minute walk from the parking area, was easily accessible by foot.

I had made this trek many times with our group and was familiar with the small stream and grassy knoll that marked our path. (I was also delighted by our sporadic encounters with a woodcock that had chosen to nest there.) Confident that I could make my way into and out of the woods without the aid of our guides, I asked my wife one day if she would like to see our camp.

We made it to the shelter in no time—a robust lean-to structure that had blanketed us from the elements not a week before. After admiring our handiwork, my wife asked if we could return to our vehicle. It was late, we hadn't had dinner, and darkness was upon us. In less than five minutes we were off course.

A mild sense of trepidation set in as I admitted that I had lost the way. Together we decided that we would find a waterway and follow it to safety. We knew that Chaffee Creek paralleled the road for long stretches and that eventually we would pass a country lane or find our way to lower ground (and with it, civilization).

We located an empty stream bed and walked along the bank. What was a trickle slowly became a babbling brook. We continued for what seemed like an eternity. Then, as suddenly as we had wandered off course, we stumbled onto a single-lane stretch of seasonal highway less than a mile from our car.

Sun Sticks

The sun stick (also known as a shadow compass) is an age-old technique that helps determine north, south, east, and west much like a standard

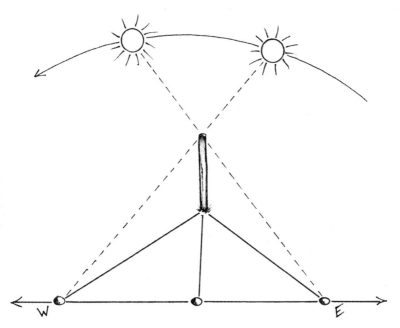

The sun stick is an indispensable navigational tool.

compass. When the sun is out, insert a straight stick into the ground. Do this in a place that is flat and open to the sun. With a stone, mark the end of the shadow cast by your stick. Every fifteen minutes or so, add a new stone to mark the location of the stick's shadow. Connect the dots that mark the shadow's course and you'll find that you have a straight line running from east to west. (The first marker that you placed represents west and your final mark represents east.) Your north/south axis can then be drawn in at a ninety-degree angle to your east/west line.

Knowing your direction can help you determine which way to go. If, for example, you know that you came in from the south and are likely to run into a road if you travel in that direction, you now have an idea of which direction to walk.

▼▼▼

Maps, Compasses, and Global Positioning System Units

Modern tools such as maps, compasses, and GPS units are of little value if you don't know how to use them. While each of these pieces of equipment should be considered survival gear, remember that batteries can die and high-tech gadgetry can fail.

MAPS

Although I don't always carry them, I prefer the use of topographic maps. These utilize contour lines to give you an idea of the terrain you are likely to encounter, such as slopes, ridges, and valleys. If you are hiking in an area where the trail is well defined, posted trail maps are often sufficient. If you are traveling in an area with which you are unfamiliar (or the trail is not well defined), these are indispensable.

COMPASSES

The easiest way to use a pathfinder compass in the United States is to identify magnetic north. To do so, line up your orienting arrow with the red end of your magnetic needle. Because the earth's magnetic field shifts, however, this does not always correspond with what is known as true north, which is marked on topographic maps with a star.

Magnetic north can vary greatly depending on your location but will give you some indication of your intended course. If you find yourself lost on a hike bearing north, for example, simply reverse your direction and bear south.

GLOBAL POSITIONING SYSTEM UNITS

GPS units use satellite signals to identify your position on earth. Although they are incredibly accurate, I don't often rely on them. GPS units are no substitute for true navigational skills, as they can easily become lost or damaged.

Staying Found and the Story Trail

How about not getting lost in the first place? In Jon Young's "Seeing through Native Eyes" audio series, he talks about what is known as the Story Trail. This method has been used in many different ways by native peoples over the ages to instruct, encourage awareness, and bequeath information. In its most elementary form, the Story Trail is a way to ensure that you remain cognizant of where you are by noting prominent landmarks or anything in the landscape that piques your interest.

In Young's telling of how the Story Trail can work, he speaks about an inner-city youth who was able to successfully walk into and out of the New Jersey wilderness during a lost-proofing exercise. While visiting her grandmother in Puerto Rico, this student had been instructed to make up a story when she traveled into the jungle from the things that she found along the way. By using this simple technique, she observed her surroundings and when it was time to turn around, told her story in reverse.

I find that as a practitioner of primitive skills I am constantly searching for ways to immerse myself in the environment. I might look at a track, peer into a hollow cavity, listen to birds, or collect material for cordage. In this way I am creating my own story. Instead of quickly hiking through an area, oblivious to the changes around me, I am involved, connected, and aware and therefore much less likely to become lost.

▲▲▲▲

153

Exercises

1. Visit a local trailhead and peruse the register. Of those who have chosen to sign in, how many provided their name, the date, and time of arrival? If you were part of a search-and-rescue team, would you have any indication, based on the details provided, of each individual's proposed course?

2. Experiment with using different materials to create a signal fire, noting the density and color of the smoke you produce. In addition, use a

sun stick to chart an east-west line. Check this against a compass for accuracy.

3. Take a walk in the woods with the intention of getting off course. Using one of the methods described above, attempt to successfully navigate your way back to civilization. *I advise that you do this only if you have a reasonable backup plan in place—in other words, you have the resources at your disposal to find your way out independently.*

Conclusion

Every tree wore a thick cloak of white, every stump and boulder a
jaunty snowy cap, and there was that perfect, immense stillness that
you get nowhere else but in a big woods after a heavy snowfall.

Bill Bryson, *A Walk in the Woods*

It is one of my deepest and sincerest hopes that this book not only
saves lives but helps to reconnect others with the natural world. I have
also intended this book to fill a void in the literature, thereby strengthen-
ing the path that so many of us travel in an attempt to reclaim the skills
of our forebears.

My own forays, accompanied by the many youth and adult groups that
I have led on winter outings, have been overwhelmingly joyous occasions.
Despite the hard work that building a group shelter requires, there is
much laughter and merriment as we embark on these adventures.

The winter experience need not be met with apprehension. Fear comes
from a lack of connection, something that can be alleviated only through
steady practice. I encourage you to start your journey now, one step at a
time. You'll be amazed at the transformation that occurs once you learn
to become more self-reliant. Once you master this skill, no one can take
it away from you.

It is important to remember that learning these skills takes time. There
is no need to venture far from the safety of a warm dwelling on your first
few campouts. Work with primitive fire devices as much as you can, but

always carry modern methods. Fire is too critical to not have a backup.

With my own groups, not only do I know the strengths of each of my participants, but I invite only those who have tested their mettle at our weekly meetings. I need to see that a student is persistent, dedicated, and above all able to carry his or her own weight. I look to those who are team players and who do not pose any behavioral risks. I have found over the years that many of my participants who have had trouble in school, either socially or academically, shine when they arrive at my program. We learn through trial and error. There are no easy rewards, and the experience is holistic.

When it comes to working with groups who have never slept in a snow shelter, I'm always sure to be within close proximity of a warm space. Although I make this decision principally to quell parental concerns, I have yet to find the need to take refuge in an indoor space with any of my groups.

On rookie outings I often bring along several bales of hay. (By the end of the day, most groups don't have the stamina to gather enough bedding to insulate their bodies from the ground.) Spreading out the contents of a bale of hay is a quick and easy way to ensure a comfortable night's sleep. As the proficiency of my students increases, so does the intensity of these outings.

It is with the above in mind that Jon and I ventured into the wilderness. Here he picks up the narrative:

> On the morning of Saturday, February 8, 2014, Dave and I embarked on an excursion into the wilds of Danby State Forest in Danby, New York. Primitive Pursuits instructor Dave Muska also accompanied us on this trip. The Wednesday before our departure, winter storm Nika blanketed our region in almost a foot of snow. Although it was bitterly cold (temperatures at night fell into the single digits), conditions for daytime shelter building were ideal.
>
> Our goal was to simulate a day hike gone awry, proving that the skills espoused in this book could sustain the lives of

three outdoorsmen over the course of twenty-four hours under adverse conditions. We set off under the guise of a trio of unsuspecting backpackers with no intention of getting lost. Although dressed appropriately for the conditions, we brought along few tools and only a modest amount of food and water. We also dispensed with certain amenities, including sleeping bags. If disaster struck, we were close enough to our vehicles (a twenty-minute walk) to seek aid.

We began early enough in the day that we had adequate light for the procurement of shelter-building materials. Muska and I arrived at Dave's house at 8:00 a.m. and ascended a seasonal portion of Eastman Hill Road that, during the winter season, is regarded as a popular snowmobiling thoroughfare. As we walked, we gathered combustible materials for our tinder bundle—goldenrod, birch bark, and punk. The latter we amassed in large quantities; the pockets of my jacket overflowed with crumbling, fibrous wood fragments.

When we reached the top of the hill, Dave took an abrupt left onto a portion of the Finger Lakes Trail, a network of continuous footpaths stretching across the state. We then left the trail and passed an old stone foundation and abandoned well. My mind turned to thoughts of the region's first settlers, who had arrived in 1795, and the challenge of persevering under such harsh winter conditions.

We chose a spot about one hundred yards off the trail overlooking a ravine. Because warmth was not an immediate concern, Dave suggested we begin work on our shelter. We found a plateau bordering a dense patch of spruce and gathered beams for the construction of a snow tepee. Dave interlocked a series of Y beams as Muska and I looked on. We positioned more beams to complete the shelter's frame and began shoveling in earnest.

By 11:00 we had finished work on the main shelter and began to explore the ravine for crafting and fire-building materials. Not five minutes into our walk, we happened on a bramble of rose hips. A graduate of the College of Environmental Science and Forestry in Syracuse, Muska quickly identified these by their Latin name. "Rosa canina," he said, popping a handful of berries into his mouth.

We found running water at the base of the ravine, but because there was no way to ensure it was free from contaminants, we continued on. Muska walked to the other side of the stream while Dave and I worked our way toward higher ground.

We made note of a large aspen that had broken in half and collected a splinter for use as a baseboard in our friction kit. Then, as I peeled bark slabs from an aging tree to house our tinder, Dave felled a white pine and threw it over his shoulder.

Muska, who despite his modest stature has the strength of a musk ox, emerged from a thicket carrying aspen branches and pieces of varnish shelf fungus—a flat, polypore mushroom that makes a wonderful coal extender. We trudged through the snow back to our camp.

We began work on the fire shortly before noon. First, Muska whittled a section of his aspen branch into a spindle. After removing the bark, he gently tapered the ends before smoothing the midsection. He then tapped his knife into a poplar branch, splitting it in half. This he set aside as his handhold.

Producing a length of cord from his pocket, Dave wrapped the spindle while Muska bored a hole in the aspen baseboard. I watched as Dave made long pulls with the cord and smoke poured from the socket.

Dave sliced a notch in the baseboard while Muska stuffed spruce needles into the handhold for lubrication. Our tinder, which comprised punky wood, birch bark, and aspen shavings, sat on a curve of pine bark to my right. I clutched a bundle of fine, wispy spruce branches to my chest. Within moments a coal appeared beneath the notch.

Muska emptied the coal into our tinder bundle and gently

exhaled. Smoke billowed from between his hands, but flame eluded us. In fewer than five minutes our hopes of fire were extinguished. It was 1:00 in the afternoon.

I took a leak and noticed that my urine was a dark yellow color. I was becoming dehydrated. I sipped from a bottle of water I had in my pack but was careful to ration this precious resource. Already its contents had cooled such that portions of the bottle were frozen. Fire was quickly becoming a necessity.

We discussed the reasons for losing the coal. "Our tinder's too damp," Dave concluded. Before attempting another coal, he gathered more punk and some dry beech leaves, pressing them into a nest. Muska and I produced another coal, but again our bundle proved insufficient.

We took a break from fire making to continue work on the shelter. As Muska excavated and hollowed the core of our snow tepee, Dave and I collected bedding materials. In addition to large boughs for our frame, we gathered armfuls of spruce braches to create an airy mattress.

We continued our work on the friction kit, to no avail. It was 4:30 and the sun had begun its descent. Noting the palpable sense of urgency we now faced, Dave pulled one of his trusted Bic lighters from his pocket and handed it to me. "You do the honors," he said. I held the flame under a bundle of spruce twigs and for the first time in more than eight hours felt true warmth.

We quickly added kindling and our modest flame grew into a raging inferno. Dave placed a length of white pine next to the fire to warm the bark. After fifteen minutes he tapped his knife along the tree, moisture bleeding from the incisions.

Dave carved a flat, spatula-like instrument and methodically removed the bark from the tree. As he did so, we sampled pieces of the cambium, or inner bark, which had a pleasant taste and the consistency of gum. Once his sheet was removed, he harvested a maple sapling and, careful to split the wood near knots in the branch, fashioned clips for his container. The bark sheet, which was pliable, was easily manipulated to fold at the corners. The clips completed the basket.

Dave filled his container with snow and placed it on some branches near the edge of the fire. As he did so, I retrieved a metal cup from my pack and, using needles from the white pine, brewed a warm tea. I passed a bag of trail mix around the fire as my two companions shared stories of past forays into the wild.

I could see Orion overhead, clear and lustrous. A sudden call interrupted the stillness: "Who cooks for you? Who cooks for you all?" It was the barred owl, its eerie cry echoing over the ravine like a distant memory.

After drinking and warming our bodies near the fire, we set off on an evening hike, keeping our headlamps trained on the intricate web of tracks intersecting our path. Before long we encountered deer, shrew, and a bounding predator that, because the snow was so deep, was difficult to identify. "Fisher, perhaps," Dave surmised.

Even though I had two pairs of wool socks and insulated winter boots, I was no match for the elements. Dave's thermometer read ten degrees, and this only strengthened my resolve to return to the comfort of the fire. By the time we made it back to our camp, my toes were stinging with pain. Dave instructed me to remove my boots and placed spruce limbs on the ground before me. "Put your feet on these," he said. Within minutes the pain had abated.

It was time to turn in. Before leaving the fire, Muska pulled a chocolate bar from his backpack and split it three ways. He and I crawled into the shelter as Dave quarried blocks and handed them to us to stack near the entrance. At 10:30 p.m. we closed the door.

Our spruce mattress was wonderfully aromatic. I breathed deeply as my eyes fixed on the faint light of the moon peeking through the cracks in the door. It was clear our shelter was of sound design—I was able to lie down without my feet or head touching the walls.

For as much repose as our shelter provided, I was not accustomed to such lodgings and sleep proved difficult. We dozed intermittently until 2:30 a.m., when Dave turned on his headlamp and glanced at the thermometer. Suspended from a beam above our heads, it read a comfortable forty degrees. Satisfied that our experiment was a success (and knowing that we would be more comfortable by the fire), Dave kicked out the door and we issued forth into the night.

I hung the thermometer on a nearby branch and checked it again at 3:00. The temperature had fallen to five degrees. This was a remarkable achievement. Our shelter, which comprised nothing more than snow, beams, and branches, had maintained a disparity of thirty-five degrees with the outside world.

A light snow fell as the mercury continued to drop. The breeze shifted, blowing smoke into my eyes. As we huddled around the fire, I adjusted my position on the log I was using as a bench and asked the question I had been holding on to all evening.

"Why do you do this?" I said.

"For me, it's about self-sufficiency," Dave said. "It's the feeling that I've done something productive." He flashed a mischievous smile. "Besides, what else are you going to do? Watch television?"

Muska concurred, adding, "It gives me an appreciation for the simplest of things. I mean, I'm amazed by running water."

I knew what he meant. As much as I had enjoyed our stay, I knew I would never again take the comfort of modern conveniences for granted.

Dave assembled a crude bed of logs and curled up next to the fire. Muska laid out his sleeping pad and leaned back against a fallen tree. Tired but alert, I tended the flames until daybreak.

Conclusion

I checked the thermometer one last time as the sun crept over the horizon. It read one degree. At 7:00 we gathered our belongings, put out the fire, and began the slog back to civilization.

For anyone planning on leading groups into the wilderness, I encourage you to start slowly. Include a multitude of easy-to-prepare, energy-rich foods. Position yourself near a reliable source of water, and keep a pot of tea warming by the fire. Know your participants and make sure they bring appropriate gear.

Although this book focuses on the most critical aspects of winter survival, there is an array of skills that encompass our collective ancestry that are not season-to-season specific. This includes tanning, weaponry, primitive cooking, pottery, awareness skills, and learning to interpret bird language. Simply put, the more you know, the better off you'll be. In appendix D I have included a list of books that will guide you on the path toward becoming a more confident and connected outdoorsman. I have also included classic survivalist fiction such as Gary Paulsen's *Hatchet* and *My Side of the Mountain* by Jean Craighead George.

I encourage you to be creative, keep your priorities in the forefront of your mind, and above all, have fun!

Appendix A

Motor Vehicle Considerations

In the fall of 2006, James Kim and his family left their home in San Francisco for a Thanksgiving trip to the Pacific Northwest. After they departed from Seattle, the family's vehicle became stranded near a canyon in the remote Oregon wilderness. Despite being ill prepared, Kim left his wife, Kati, and daughters, Penelope and Sabine, in an effort to seek aid. His body was discovered more than a week later. Rescuers and medical experts determined that Kim, who had wandered more than ten miles from the family's vehicle, had become disoriented from hypothermia.[1]

In recent years, changing weather patterns have caught more and more people off guard as winter storms knock out utilities and strand motorists on roadways. Beyond the fundamentals of winter survival, stranded motorist emergencies have their own unique considerations. Learning to prepare for the unexpected can help you make the most of an emergency. The same priorities that apply to wilderness settings need to be respected in these situations.

Problems

Vehicles often provide us with a false sense of security. As we drive from one place to another, it's easy to forget that we're traveling through wilderness areas, and as a result, we neglect to take appropriate precautions.

Mechanical failure, accidents, or inclement weather may throw travelers into unexpected survival situations.

I recommend that you dress (or pack) as if you were going to have to leave your vehicle. I do this even when I'm traveling from home to work and back. It's only a twenty-five-minute commute, but I know how quickly winter conditions can turn ugly. Another incentive for having the right clothing is that cell phones don't always work. Even though I live in an area that is moderately populated, there are dead zones where cell phones don't receive service. Coincidentally, one of these zones happens to be in an isolated area that historically gets significant snowfall and where roadway conditions are treacherous.

Be wary of GPS units and online directions. People have relied on modern travel aids and found themselves on country roads (or even seasonal highways) well off the beaten path. Where I live, I caution people not to use GPS units to find their way to our home. More than once people have been directed to go up an unmaintained dirt road that, even in the summer, is best handled by a four-wheel-drive vehicle.

Prevention

When embarking on a road trip, let someone know of your travel plans. Be sure to relay your timeline, travel route, make, model, license plate number, and color of your vehicle, as well as the names and ages of everyone in your party. The best person to tell is the person you're going to visit. Telling a friend at home is also advisable, but he or she won't miss you if your arrival is delayed. Stay in touch with your destination if you're running late or choose to alter your route. The idea here is that if you do become stranded, your contact will be able to aid in any search-and-rescue efforts.

Before any trip, be sure to check the weather. Many stranded-vehicle situations could be avoided if motorists not only checked the weather before departing but stayed home or on vacation an extra day. Vehicles are only so capable. Submit to Mother Nature's power and stay away from roadways when it seems like the sensible thing to do.

In addition to bringing clothing that will shelter you from the elements if you need to work outside or travel on foot, it is wise to have extra survival gear in your vehicle. My family takes only a few big road trips each winter, but I have a box of items that will assist us in meeting our needs if the unexpected arises. This includes a shovel, extra food, blankets, a means of procuring water, and fire starters. A complete list of recommended items is covered in appendix B.

What to Do If You Are Stranded

If you are stranded, the same fundamental needs that you would encounter in a wilderness-based situation apply here. The difference is that you can use your vehicle to your advantage. A vehicle offers refuge from wind and precipitation and is a space that, to an extent, will maintain heat. (If your car still starts, heat may be less of an issue.) Use this resource wisely. Keeping warm is your number one priority. Wear extra clothes, use blankets and sleeping bags if you have them, and use your heater conservatively.

165

For the Unprepared

Years ago I saw Tom Brown Jr. and several of his instructors from the Tracker School on one of the morning news shows. Among other things, Tom and his team illustrated how a car could be stuffed full of leaves, using it as a container much like a leaf crib. This is an excellent idea if insulating materials are available.

To avoid exhausting your fuel supply, exercise caution when running your vehicle to maintain warmth. The following ideas will help bolster your automobile's sheltering capabilities and will serve you well if you become stranded.

As you have already learned, snow is an excellent insulator when used in shelter construction. There have been many times when I have camped out in my vehicle in the winter. My minivan works well for this, and I have always been prepared with a good sleeping mat and winter sleeping bag. Vehicles can get cold. Without heat, added insulation, or proper camping gear, a night spent in a vehicle can be extremely uncomfortable.

One way to improve the insulating property of your car is to cover it in a thick layer of snow, essentially using your vehicle as the core of a snow shelter. Cars are made of metal and varying degrees of insulation but are not necessarily constructed with the survivalist in mind. My own van, for instance, has small holes in the internal frame where the seats can be adjusted that lead directly to the outside. Cold seeps into our cars. Turning your car into a snow shelter will increase its value immensely.

I tested this theory in the aftermath of winter storm Hercules in January of 2014. My older son and I spent several hours inside my Prius, which we had enveloped in a foot of snow. (We erected an A-frame entrance near the driver's side door so we could get in and out with ease.) With outside temperatures holding steady at minus seven degrees Fahrenheit, we surprisingly found comfort—in our shelter the inside temperature quickly warmed to thirty degrees.

I was able to sit while dressed in a sensible winter outfit and work barehanded without incident. We stayed outside for several hours, and I eventually fell asleep. Satisfied with our experiment, at 1:30 a.m. we returned to the warmth of our home.

I cannot overemphasize the value of using your vehicle in this way. If we had been outside and exposed to the elements, we would have faced a wind chill of close to minus twenty-five degrees. Your vehicle is a lifesaving option that is not to be overlooked.

To follow up on our experiment, I wanted to see how warm our car would get under similar conditions without the aid of snow. I was fortunate that less than a week later, on the heels of winter storm Ion, I awoke to temperatures of minus six. When I entered the Prius—this time accompanied by my faithful Labradoodle, Pearl—I measured the inside temperature at minus nine degrees.

During our hour-long experiment, outside temperatures remained fairly constant with almost no wind. Our interior temperature rose to a meager 3.6 degrees. This was admittedly difficult to endure. My hands ached and I found it almost impossible to take notes. If you used a car in this way while in the throes of a true survival situation (and under similar conditions without the aid of insulation), it would indeed be a painful, albeit lifesaving, experience.

When using your vehicle in this way, there are several key safety factors to keep in mind:

- ▲ Don't run your car if it is covered in snow. Exhaust may flood the interior space, resulting in asphyxiation.
- ▲ Be sure to ventilate. A car doesn't breathe like a snow shelter, so be sure to leave a window cracked. Whenever I've turned my vehicle into the core of a snow shelter, I've made sure that I can still open one door, which leads to a covered alcove.
- ▲ Mark or flag your location. Once your vehicle is covered in snow, it will be all but impossible for rescuers to see. Use orange flagging on poles or whatever is available to make it easier for searchers to see you. Think contrast when marking your location. Use colors and shapes that are out of place in the natural environment.

Solar Gain

On milder days with a clear sky, sunlight can add heat to your vehicle because of the greenhouse effect. From my kitchen window I have observed ice melt off my windshield as the morning sun crept over the hillside and have enjoyed a warm car even though it was below freezing outside. During my own trials I have recorded temperatures above fifty degrees in my car, even though the outside temperature was twenty. On a day that hovered around the freezing mark, the inside temperature of my vehicle reached seventy-five.

Exposing the windows of your vehicle to the sun for the purpose of solar gain is something to consider. Overall outside temperatures, wind, and sun exposure should all be taken into account when making this decision. If you've determined that exposing your windows to the sun is beneficial, simply cover them again with snow as night descends.

The Need for Fire

A fire should be made for several reasons—it will help keep you warm and can be used as a signaling device. Be sure to keep a large pile of evergreen boughs nearby so you can feed your fire if the need arises.

The heat from a fire can also be brought into your vehicle by heating rocks. Be sure to place these on something that won't ignite if they're too hot to handle. One way to do this is to pile unheated rocks on the floor of your vehicle, and then place your hot rocks on top.

During the writing of this book, a family of six survived two days in the Nevada Mountains utilizing this method. According to NBC News reports, James Glanton built a fire inside a spare tire, used brush for kindling, and brought heated rocks back to his vehicle. With temperatures reaching more than twenty degrees below zero, "his ingenuity was hailed as the difference between life and death."[2]

Without the aid of a lighter or matches, a car itself can be used to make fire. Cigarette lighters, which aren't always present in today's vehicles, are an obvious choice. Punky wood, for example, can be easily ignited with a cigarette lighter. If your vehicle doesn't have a cigarette lighter, they can often be purchased to fit your make and model.

Fire can be made using a car battery, a set of jumper cables, and a pencil. This sounds like a bit of a parlor trick, but it works. Expose the lead on both ends of your pencil by gently carving away the wood. Attach the positive and negative claws from one end of your jumper cables so that the metal portion comes into contact with the graphite. Then place your pencil in a pile of tinder. Connect the other positive and negative ends of your jumper cables to the battery and start your vehicle. This should ignite your pile of tinder. I have even created sparks using jumper cables to light tinder fungus and punky wood.

Steel wool can be set to smolder simply by teasing it out so it's long enough to touch the positive and negative points of your battery. In moments your steel wool will begin to smolder. Simply place this in a tinder bundle and coax into flame.

Water

Your body's need for proper hydration doesn't change when you're stranded with your vehicle. One benefit to creating water with a car is that, assuming you have a catch, snow can be melted on your dashboard or with hot rocks.

Pirating Your Vehicle

The considerations that factor into making the decision of whether or not to walk out were addressed in chapter 7. The difference here, of course, is that you have the added advantage of pirating your car for resources.

In a classic episode of *I Shouldn't Be Alive*, Les Stroud took on the challenge of reenacting a famous modern-day survival story that unfolded in the high desert of Nevada. In December of 1993, James and Jennifer Stolpa and their five-month-old infant, Clayton, became stranded near the Charles Sheldon National Wildlife Refuge. The family barely made it out alive, hiking for more than forty-eight hours and sacrificing their toes to frostbite in an attempt to find safety.[3]

In Stroud's version of the ordeal, he made use of his vehicle before setting off across the barren landscape. He beefed up his footwear by removing the insulated seating, grabbed a hub cap for digging, and tore out wires to use as binding and potential snares. As a skilled survivalist, Stroud knew what he was up against and used his vehicle to successfully meet this challenge. In a true survival situation, don't be afraid to pirate your vehicle. Cars can be replaced. Your life cannot.

One thing to keep in mind when walking away from a motor vehicle is that, if you're unsure as to where the road in front of you might lead, heading back in the direction from which you came is a logical course of action.

Appendix B

Survival Kits

Although I'm a strong proponent of learning primitive survival skills, modern-day survival kits are important, especially within the context of a winter survival situation. A survival kit is a small package of indispensable, tested gear that will help you meet your needs if the situation arises. This kit should be small enough that it can be on your person at all times. My daily kit comprises a Bic lighter and a quality folding knife. I have these items with me wherever I go. When I'm planning an outdoor adventure or leading a group into the wilderness, my kit reflects not only standard survival needs but my proficiency and the environment in which I'm traveling. Of course, the materials that I bring with me in the event of an unexpected "What if?" situation on a winter mountain hike will be different from the materials I bring during a summer canoe trip.

In college when I led winter camping trips into the High Peaks of New York's Adirondack Mountains, our "survival kit" was a bit large and anticipated the needs of an immobilized hiker. In addition to items that would assist in making fire and shelter, we carried enough gear on our day hikes from camp to ensure that an injured hiker and a companion could stay in an exposed environment in comfort while aid was sought. This meant bringing a small cooking stove and pot, extra food and tea, a sleeping bag, bivouac sack, and ground pad. Although we never needed this gear (which went beyond the parameters of a typical survival kit), it provided peace of mind and showed that we understood that for the unprepared, things could turn ugly.

I've been in the High Peaks when temperatures were thirty below zero. This, coupled with a strong wind, made the temperature feel more like fifty below. On one particular hike after summiting Wright Peak, I removed my mittens to retrieve something from my pack. Instantly my hands ached with cold and became numb. I remember wondering how long someone would last if he fractured a leg. This recognition of the harsh realities one might face during an unexpected night in the wilderness influences what I bring with me on every outing.

A survival kit is not only a reflection of your skill set; it is a tool to help address specific needs that your environment presents. A comprehensive kit will aid you in procuring vital, fundamental resources to meet the challenges of a worst-case scenario. If you happen to be an expert fire maker who has experience finding and using punky wood and you feel comfortable making fire under the worst of conditions, you may decide that carrying Vaseline-saturated cotton balls isn't necessary. A backcountry kit should be small enough that you can keep it on your person at all times. Ultimately it is up to you to decide what goes in. Test your gear before you need it! Beware of cheap survival products that are nothing more than gimmicks. Below are suggestions for items that should go into your kit, along with explanations.

- ▲ FIRE MAKERS: I like to bring three different modern fire-making methods when I'm heading outdoors. Fire is too valuable for you not to have redundancy in this department. Over the years I have carried Bic lighters, matches, sparking tools, fire pistons, and flint and steel sets.
- ▲ KNIFE: A quality full-tang knife is invaluable in any wilderness setting. In fact, you may want to consider carrying two knives. I like to carve using a Mora (orange is a good color) and will often carry a heavier "beater" knife for chopping and heavy use. My favorite is the Ka-Bar Kukri, or if I want to carry something more streamlined, I use my Cold Steel Bushman.

- **SMALL FOLDING SAW:** Purchase a high-end folding saw from your local farm and garden store. These are lightweight and quite useful.
- **REFLECTOR BLANKET:** A good emergency blanket is worth its weight in gold. These are best used as heat reflectors in front of a fire. In addition, they are waterproof, and the orange side can be used for signaling. I prefer Heatsheets made by Adventure Medical Kits. You may consider carrying more than one reflector blanket—one for your personal needs, the other to mark your location.
- **FIRE STARTERS:** These will help you to get a fire going, especially in wet or windy conditions. If you decide this is something you want to carry, they can be made at home by mixing cotton balls in Vaseline. These are best stored in a small plastic container. Once lit, these will burn well for several minutes, enabling you to dry out kindling and get your fire going.
- **HAND/BODY WARMERS:** I've come to see the value in these lightweight items. They could mean the difference between frostbitten hands and keeping your fingers warm enough to accomplish critical, dexterous tasks.
- **SMALL SHOVEL:** This is an item that is clearly too large to fit in a small pack but should nevertheless be considered a prime piece of survival gear to carry on any winter excursion. Some high-end mountaineering shovels contain a snow saw in the handle. I typically use a shovel designed to fit into a car trunk.
- **SMALL AX:** Gerber makes a nice mini-ax (Paxe) that fits easily into a larger pack. The one I have has a knife stored in the hollow handle.
- **CORDAGE:** I carry fishing line, heavy-duty hemp twine, and hundred-pound test nylon rope. Consider all your potential needs when it comes to cordage.
- **METAL CUP:** For use in drinking and boiling water.
- **FISHING KIT:** In addition to monofilament, you should carry an assortment of hooks, weights, lures, and jigs that are suitable

for ice fishing.

- ▲ **PEANUT BUTTER:** This is not food for you but bait to produce food. I recommend individual serving-sized packets that come wrapped in foil. I'm always concerned about food smells mingling in my pack (which will only attract rodents), so I encourage you to wrap these again in plastic wrap or aluminum foil and store them within a plastic, zipper-lock bag.
- ▲ **FOOD:** What you choose should be dense and energy-rich (nuts, seeds, jerky). Take the same precautions as above when storing food in your pack. I have carried Jell-O mix, which can be used to make a hot drink. This may help energize someone suffering from hypothermia.
- ▲ **HEADLAMP:** Headlamps are compact and enable you to keep both hands free. Always bring extra batteries.
- ▲ **CELL PHONE:** This is a good thing to have with you during any foray into the wilderness. If you're in a dead area, consider turning off your phone and turning it back on periodically to see if you have a signal. (Cell phone batteries will drain quickly if they are searching for a signal.)
- ▲ **MAP AND COMPASS:** These important items should accompany you on any backcountry adventure. Take the time to learn how to use these fundamental navigational tools.
- ▲ **WHISTLE:** Three short whistle blasts repeated every minute will indicate a need for help. These travel farther than the human voice.
- ▲ **ORANGE FLAGGING:** Flagging is wonderful for signaling, trail markers, and marking your shelter.
- ▲ **FIRST AID KIT:** In addition to a first aid kit, I recommend taking a basic first aid and CPR course.
- ▲ **DUCT TAPE:** One hundred and one uses. Don't leave home without it.
- ▲ **HEAVY-DUTY GARBAGE BAGS:** Many uses. Garbage bags can be turned into shelter, stuffed with leaves, or used to create a

makeshift poncho, protecting you from wind and rain.

The Car Kit

Vehicles will protect you from wind and precipitation but can be cold. Treat your vehicle as if it were a tent and remember to dress and bring clothes intended to tackle a worst-case scenario.

In addition to those items listed above, consider

- Winter sleeping bag
- Sleeping pad
- Extra water
- Jumper cables
- Pencils for starting fire (see appendix A)
- Camping stove with fuel
- Cooking kit
- Food/MRE (meals ready to eat) (choose dried, energy-rich food that's easy to prepare)
- Tire chains
- Come-along with strong rope or additional cable
- Larger shovel
- Tarp
- Rope
- Flares
- Global positioning system unit (see cautions about GPS units in chapter 7 and appendix A)

Appendix C

Winter Gear Checklist

Below is the gear list I provide participants for our winter overnights in the Primitive Pursuits program. Although this book espouses skills that will ultimately enable one to survive independent of gear, I always advise having certain resources at your disposal. Refer to this checklist when preparing to venture into the outdoors.

- ▲ A nonfolding knife with a blade no longer than four inches
- ▲ Matches or lighter
- ▲ Spoon, bowl, and cup
- ▲ Shovel
- ▲ Sleeping bag and sleeping pad
- ▲ A ground cloth (tarp or plastic sheet)
- ▲ Two warm top layers, noncotton
- ▲ Two noncotton sweaters
- ▲ Three pairs of wool socks
- ▲ Winter boots
- ▲ Two pairs of pants, noncotton

- Two pairs of long underwear, noncotton
- Winter jacket
- Snow pants
- Two pairs of gloves or mittens
- A warm hat or balaclava
- Ski goggles
- Extra underwear
- Toothbrush and toothpaste
- Flashlight or headlamp
- Batteries
- Four feet of strong cordage
- Toilet paper
- Nonperishable food and water
- A three-day supply of any prescribed daily medications
- Optional: Snow shoes, cross country skis, field guides, camera

Appendix D

Suggested Reading

Blankenship, Bart, and Robin Blankenship. *Earth Knack: Stone Age Skills for the 21st Century*. Salt Lake City: Peregrine Smith, 1996.

Brown, Tom, Jr., with Brandt Morgan. *Tom Brown's Field Guide to Nature Observation and Tracking*. New York: Berkley, 1986.

Bryson, Bill. *A Walk in the Woods*. New York: Anchor Books, 1998.

Frost, Robert. *Robert Frost: Selected Poems*. New York: Gramercy Books, 1992.

George, Jean Craighead. *My Side of the Mountain*. New York: Penguin, 1959.

Gibbons, Diane K. *Mammal Tracks and Sign of the Northeast*. Hanover, NH: University Press of New England, 2003.

Murie, Olaus J., and Mark Elbroch. *Peterson Field Guide to Animal Tracks. 3rd ed.* New York: Houghton Mifflin Harcourt, 2005.

Paulsen, Gary. *Hatchet*. New York: Simon & Schuster, 1987.

Read, Piers Paul. *Alive*. New York: Harper Collins, 1974.

Rezendes, Paul. *Tracking and the Art of Seeing: How to Read Animal Tracks and Sign*. New York: Harper Collins, 1999.

Stokes, Donald W. *A Guide to Nature in Winter: Northeast and North Central North America*. Boston: Little, Brown, 1976.

Thayer, Samuel. *The Forager's Harvest: A Guide to Identifying,*

Harvesting, and Preparing Edible Wild Plants. Ogema, WI: Forager's Harvest, 2006.

Young, Jon. *What the Robin Knows: How Birds Reveal the Secrets of the Natural World.* New York: Houghton Mifflin, 2013.

Notes

Introduction

1. Samuel Thayer, *Nature's Garden: A Guide to Identifying, Harvesting, and Preparing Edible Wild Plants* (Ogema, WI: Forager's Harvest Press, 2010), 21.

2. Intergovernmental Panel on Climate Change, "Headline Statements from the Summary for Policymakers," http://www.ipcc.ch/news_and_events/docs/ar5/ar5_wg1_headlines.pdf.

3. National Wildlife Federation, "Odd-ball Winter Weather: Global Warming's Wake-up Call for the Northern United States," http://www.nwf.org/pdf/Global-Warming/NWF_WinterWeather_Medium_REV.pdf.

4. National Aeronautics and Space Administration (NASA), "Global Climate Change: Causes," http://climate.nasa.gov/causes.

5. Geoffrey Mohan, "Carbon Dioxide Levels in Atmosphere Pass 400 Milestone, Again," *Los Angeles Times*, May 20, 2013.

6. Doyle Rice and Doug Stanglin, "Winter Storm Hits Northeast with Heavy Snow, Wind," *USA Today*, January 3, 2014.

7. Larry Copeland, Doyle Rice, and Doug Stanglin, "Deep South Shuts Down as Rare Snow, Ice Hit Region," *USA Today*, January 29, 2014.

Chapter 1

1. Tom Brown Jr., with Brandt Morgan, *Tom Brown's Field Guide to Wilderness Survival.* (New York: Berkley, 1983), 11.

2. Jim Suhr and Jim Salter, "Illinois Man, Sons Die in Freezing Rain on Missouri Trail," Associated Press, January 14, 2013.

3. Mayo Clinic, "Diseases and Conditions: Hypothermia." http://www.mayoclinic.org/diseases-conditions/hypothermia/basics/symptoms/con-20020453.

Chapter 2

1. Gary H. Lincoff, *National Audubon Society Field Guide to North American Mushrooms* (New York: Knopf, 1981), 467.

Chapter 3

1. Mike Lynch, "Survivor Recounts Night on Marcy," *Adirondack Daily Enterprise*, February 24, 2012.

2. Ole Henrik Magga, "Diversity in Saami Terminology for Reindeer and Snow," http://www.arcticlanguages.com/papers/Magga_Reindeer_and_Snow.pdf.

3. Tom Brown Jr., with Brandt Morgan, *Tom Brown's Field Guide to Wilderness Survival* (New York: Berkley, 1983), 24.

Chapter 4

1. Rick Curtis, *The Backpacker's Field Manual: A Comprehensive Guide to Mastering Backcountry Skills* (New York: Three Rivers Press, 1998), 60.

2. Mayo Clinic, "Diseases and Conditions: Dehydration," http://www.mayoclinic.org/diseases-conditions/dehydration/basics/symptoms/con-20030056.

3. *Curtis, Backpacker's Field Manual* 84.

4. Ibid., 85.

Chapter 5

1. Samuel Thayer, *Nature's Garden: A Guide to Identifying, Harvesting, and Preparing Edible Wild Plants* (Ogema, WI: Forager's Harvest, 2010), 55.

2. George A. Petrides, *A Field Guide to Trees and Shrubs: Northeastern and North-Central United States and Southeastern and South-Central Canada* (New York: Houghton Mifflin Harcourt, 1958), 211.

3. Ibid., 200.

4. Ibid., 126.

5. Ibid., 158.

6. Petrides, *Field Guide to Trees and Shrubs*, 25.

7. Ibid., 211, 212.

8. Peterson, *Field Guide to Edible Wild Plants*, 48.

9. Ibid., 164.

10. Thayer, *Nature's Garden*, 250–55.

11. Peterson, *Field Guide to Edible Wild Plants*, 194.

12. Ibid., 38, 164.

13. Ibid., 88.

14. Ibid., 208.

15. Ibid., 176.

16. Ibid., 112.

17. Ibid., 188.

18. Ibid., 72.

19. Ibid., 204.
20. Ibid., 166.
21. Ibid., 228.
22. Ibid., 236.
23. Ibid., 106.
24. Ibid., 168.
25. Ibid., 214.
26. Ibid., 166.
27. Ibid., 28.
28. Ibid., 52, 114.
29. Petrides, *Field Guide to Trees and Shrubs*, 246.
30. Peterson, *Field Guide to Edible Wild Plants*, 64.
31. Ibid., 224.
32. Thayer, *Nature's Garden*, 58.

Chapter 6

1. Jon Ulrich, "A Tribe Called Youth," *Life in the Finger Lakes* 13, no. 1 (Spring 2013): 54.
2. Randal Jones, "The Perfect 15-Minute Moccasin," *Wilderness Way* 3, no. 1: 38–40.
3. South Tyrol Museum of Archaeology, "The Ice Man's Clothing and Equipment: The Shoes," http://www.iceman.it/en/node/274.

▲▲▲▲

Bibliography

Brown, Tom, Jr., with Brandt Morgan. *Tom Brown's Field Guide to Wilderness Survival*. New York: Berkley, 1983.

Copeland, Larry, Doyle Rice, and Doug Stanglin. "Deep South Shuts Down as Rare Snow, Ice Hit Region." USA Today, January 29, 2014.

Curtis, Rick. *The Backpacker's Field Manual: A Comprehensive Guide to Mastering Backcountry Skills*. New York: Three Rivers Press, 1998.

Fieldstadt, Elisha, and Erin McClam. "Group That Survived Two Days in Frigid Nevada Wilderness Calls Rescuers 'Valiant.'" NBC News, December 10, 2013. http://www.nbcnews.com/news/other/group-survived-two-days-frigid-nevada-wilderness-calls-rescuers-valiant-f2D11719275.

Intergovernmental Panel on Climate Change. "Headline Statements from the Summary for Policymakers." http://www.ipcc.ch/news_and_events/docs/ar5/ar5_wg1_headlines.pdf.

Jones, Randal. "The Perfect 15-Minute Moccasin." *Wilderness Way* 3, no. 1: 38–40.

Lincoff, Gary H. *National Audubon Society Field Guide to North American Mushrooms*. New York: Knopf, 1981.

Lynch, Mike. "Survivor Recounts Night on Marcy." *Adirondack Daily Enterprise*, February 24, 2012.

Magga, Ole Henrik. "Diversity in Saami Terminology for Reindeer and Snow." http://www.arcticlanguages.com/papers/Magga_Reindeer_and_Snow.pdf.

Mayo Clinic. "Diseases and Conditions: Dehydration." http://www.mayoclinic.org/diseases-conditions/dehydration/basics/symptoms/con-20030056.

———. "Diseases and Conditions: Hypothermia." http://www.mayoclinic.org/

diseases-conditions/hypothermia/basics/symptoms/con-20020453.

Mohan, Geoffrey. "Carbon Dioxide Levels in Atmosphere Pass 400 Milestone, Again." *Los Angeles Times*, May 20, 2013.

National Aeronautics and Space Administration (NASA). "Global Climate Change: Causes." http://climate.nasa.gov/causes.

National Wildlife Federation. "Odd-ball Winter Weather: Global Warming's Wake-up Call for the Northern United States." http://www.nwf.org/pdf/Global-Warming/NWF_WinterWeather_Medium_REV.pdf.

Peterson, Lee Allen. *A Field Guide to Edible Wild Plants: Eastern and Central North America*. New York: Houghton Mifflin Harcourt, 1977.

Petrides, George A. *A Field Guide to Trees and Shrubs: Northeastern and North-Central United States and Southeastern and South-Central Canada*. New York: Houghton Mifflin Harcourt, 1958.

Rice, Doyle, and Doug Stanglin. "Winter Storm Hits Northeast with Heavy Snow, Wind." *USA Today*, January 3, 2014.

South Tyrol Museum of Archaeology. "The Ice Man's Clothing and Equipment: The Shoes." http://www.iceman.it/en/node/274.

Suhr, Jim, and Jim Salter. "Illinois Man, Sons Die in Freezing Rain on Missouri Trail." Associated Press, January 14, 2013.

Taylor, Michael. "Family Lost in Snow Tells of Their Harrowing Ordeal." *San Francisco Chronicle*, January 8, 1993.

Thayer, Samuel. *Nature's Garden: A Guide to Identifying, Harvesting, and Preparing Edible Wild Plants*. Ogema, WI: Forager's Harvest, 2010.

Ulrich, Jon. "A Tribe Called Youth." *Life in the Finger Lakes* 13, no. 1 (Spring 2013): 48–55.

Yardley, William. "Man Lost Seeking Help for Family Is Found Dead." *New York Times*, December 7, 2006.

Index

INDEX

▲▲▲▲

INDEX